THE
TRADITIONAL
HUNGARIAN KITCHEN

THE
TRADITIONAL
HUNGARIAN KITCHEN

VINCE

Hungarian original title: **Szakácskönyv**

Revised for the foreign language edition by Anikó Gergely

Translated by Hajnalka Csatorday

Translations edited by Anita Altman

Photographs by Péter Primusz, H. P. D. C.

Food preparation and styling by Tamás Lusztig (chef), Gábor Kis and György Altbäcker,

Hotel Flamenco, Budapest

Design by Judit Erdélyi

Colour Separation: 4 Color Repro, Budapest

ISBN 963 9552 45 3

Contents

Publisher's preface

This volume contains a selection of recipes from the most popular cookbook ever published in Hungary, where the name Ilona Horváth has become a household word, synonymous with the book itself. We might say, there is no household in Hungary without at least one copy. Penciled notes, dog-eared pages, grease spots prove that it is often used and not merely shelved as a collector's piece. The book is an inexhaustible source of recipes and an irrefutable reference work in matters of cooking.

Many reprints followed the first publication in 1955. The secret of this huge, even frantic, success was first credited to its timeliness. It was, after all, the first of its kind on the market, published in an era when one of the goals of omnipotent politics was to keep women away from the hearth and have them seek success in other areas of life.

Then politics and life changed and the book market was flooded with countless number of cookbooks. They were more attractive, more modern, more sophisticated, yet Hungarian women remained loyal to their "Ilona Horváth." The answer to the secret is a simple one: This cookbook is the depository of traditional Hungarian taste, generations of women have used it to recreate the flavors of "mom's cooking."

We hope that others whose cookery is based on traditions very different from ours will also find these dishes to their delight.

A few words on Hungarian cuisine

It is very difficult to give a brief description of "Hungarian cuisine". We can only speak about hundreds of thousands, millions of households and restaurants with chefs whose cooking style characterizes a small community, each with differences according to individual taste, experience, skill, and, of course, money.

Nevertheless, we shall now attempt to present a selection of some of the most distinctive features of Hungarian culinary habits, which lend an unmistakable character to our dishes independently of social status, regional differences, financial resources.

In Hungary there are three "compulsory" meals a day. Breakfast, which differs from one family to the next, from the simplest, so-called continental to a substantial one with cold cuts, bacon, sausages, eggs, cheese (and nowadays with fruit juice and cereals).

Dinner is the main meal, eaten between 12 and 2 p.m. It consists of three courses. The first is the soup introducing the meal, which is followed by the main course, usually some meat dish (or a substitute) with stewed vegetable, or meat with some garnish and salad made from fresh vegetables or pickles, or a one-course meal with or without meat and salad. The meal ends with dessert and/or fruit. Another type of dinner consists of a substantial soup followed by pasta (either salted or sweetened) and fruit.

Traditionally, Hungarian meals do not include appetizers. A choice of main courses and special desserts make a meal festive.

Stewed vegetables are the mainstay of the Hungarian diet. They are made from fresh vegetables or legumes thickened with roux or a mixture of sour cream and flour and seasoned with a variety of spices.

Traditionally, salads are not served separately, but are side dishes to meat meals and some kinds of pasta.

Evening meals, served between 7 and 8 p.m., show greater variety. Families who do not have their midday meals at home, eat dinner in the evening with the soup often left out. Others have one-course meals, still others eat cold cuts and cheese.

Hungarian meals are inconceivable without fresh, fragrant white bread with a crunchy crust. "Black bread," once synonymous with poverty, is not as common.

The use of roux or a sour cream and flour mixture to thicken dishes is a distinctive feature of Hungarian cookery.

Roux (Rántás)

Roux is made from flour fried in shortening and is often seasoned. The ratio of flour and shortening and the length of frying determine the flavor of roux and thus of the dish. "Light" roux is prepared by frying the flour until it turns white. To obtain a "rose-colored" roux, the flour is fried a little longer. "Brown" roux, cooked longer still, influences the color of the dish and also adds a distinctive taste to it.

Roux is prepared by mixing flour into hot lard (the basic ratio is 1:1, which may vary) and stirring until the desired color is obtained. Flavorings are added at this point (remember to remove the pan from the heat before you add paprika). Then comes the most critical step in the process: the adding of liquid. A small amount of cold liquid (usually 1/2-1 dl of water) is added slowly to the hot roux with constant stirring (it should not be lumpy), which is then added to the simmering food and boiled for at least 10 more minutes. If you make the roux in advance or it cools, then add hot liquid in the same ratio to make it usuable.

Thickening agent (Habarás)

Mix flour slowly and carefully, so it does not become lumpy, into sour cream, milk or egg, or a mixture of these as recommended in the recipe. Continuing to stir the paste, add first one or two tablespoons then a ladle of the hot sauce or soup being cooked. When it is smooth pour back into the pot and bring to a boil, but do not continue boiling.

Pork is the most popular meat, then fowl, primarily chicken, followed well behind by all other meat, including fish.

Even today, one or more pigs are slaughtered in nearly every village household in the winter (usually before Christmas). Processing the meat and the ensuing feast is an occasion when family and friends gather. Many urban families also buy a piglet and have it raised by relatives living in the country, in order to ensure a year's supply of meat, sausage, ham, bacon, and lard.

Smoking is the traditional method of preserving, consequently, a number of dishes acquire their distinctive flavor from smoked meat, from the dripping of smoked bacon. Smoked sausage and bacon are frequently served at the table. Furthermore, the serving of ham cooked fresh with eggs marks the end of Easter fasting.

Therefore, it follows that the use of lard is one of the most distinctive features of Hungarian cuisine. Traditionally, every dish, even most pasta and pastry, is made with lard or fried in lard, and this custom, though declining, is still very much alive. For this reason the recipes in this book specify the use of lard. However, in the majority of cases, it can be readily substituted by sunflowerseed oil, without much loss in taste.

15 g (1/2 oz) lard = 1 tablespoon oil

The time has come to mention bread spread with lard, something which is usually left out of cookbooks. There is no loyal follower of nouvelle cuisine, vegetarianism, or health food, who, if brought up in Hungary, is not tempted once in a while (by a persistent little devil named Cholesterol) to eat, just that one time, a tasty slice of bread spread with lard. Fresh bread spread with chilled lard (especially dripping of roast pork), sprinkled with salt and paprika and garnished with fresh green pepper, tomato, spring or Spanish onion, is ranked high by many in the line of gastronomic delights.

Let us now turn to food flavorings. Without doubt, paprika is the most commonly used spice. It not only flavors a great many Hungarian dishes, but also determines their color. There is a great variety available as regards spiciness and color, in fact, different regions produce different flavors – some swear by the paprika from Szeged, others by the paprika from Kalocsa – but whichever you use, use it prudently. Contrary to the widespread belief that all Hungarian food must be burning hot, it is characterized by a harmony of flavors.

Unless you use paprika to decorate food, you must stir it into hot lard

Paprika is processed to produce a variety of flavors:

SPECIAL
(különleges)
has a fine fragrance, bright red color, with a sweet or just a hint of hot taste,
it is ground very fine;

MILD
(csípősségmentes)
paprika is light red, not hot, ground medium fine;

DELICATE
(csemege)
paprika is light red, aromatic, with just a hint of hotness,
and ground medium fine;

FINE-SWEET
(édes-nemes)
is somewhat darker red, aromatic, slightly hot, and ground medium;

ROSE-RED
(rózsa)

paprika is red, hot, and ground medium;

HOT
(erős)
paprika has a color from light brown-red to yellowish,
it is very hot, and ground medium-fine.

removed from the heat (overheated paprika will turn brown and bitter) instead of sprinkling it directly into the dish.

Many dishes are made with onions. They are either cooked whole in some dishes (and removed before serving), or chopped very fine, then mostly fried or sautéed. In the latter case, it must blend into the dish thickening, adding flavor to the sauce of stews (pörkölt) and Hungarian goulash.

The fresh flavor of chopped parsley is also an indispensable ingredient of many dishes.

Green peppers and tomatoes, too, are important ingredients. Large, juicy tomatoes are used for cooking. No other kind gives quite the same result. Green peppers grown in Hungary are particularly tasty. They show a great variety ranging from dark green through yellow to red, from long to round.

The widespread use of sour cream is also very characteristic of the Hungarian kitchen. It gives a distinctive taste to many dishes and, with a few exceptions, cannot be substituted by anything else. Its quality is important.

The consumption of espresso coffee is a more recent custom adapted by every social class in the past 50 years. It is served almost as a rule after midday meals, and often during the day.

Wine is consumed traditionally, and the range of Hungarian wines is very wide. Beer is also becoming increasingly popular. Among traditional alcoholic beverages, fruit brandies are the most common. Some regions are known for their apricot brandy, others for their plum brandy.

We hope our recipes will help you create real Hungarian flavors that you will enjoy. But remember, Hungary is where you find truly authentic and tasty Hungarian dishes.

All recipes are for 4 people, except desserts, which serve 6 to 8. The recipes give both metric measurements and their closest American equivalents.

A cool oven is set at 80 °C (175 °F), a moderate oven is set at 150 - 170 °C (300 - 325 °F), a hot oven at 180 - 200 °C (350 - 400 °F), a very hot oven at 220 - 300 °C (425 - 570 °F).

SOUPS

GOULASH SOUP
(Gulyásleves)

300 g (10 1/2 oz) shank of beef

30 g (1 oz) lard

1 large onion, finely chopped

1/2 teaspoon paprika

Salt, to taste

1/2 teaspoon caraway seeds

3-4 black peppercorns

1 medium carrot, cut in quarters

1 medium parsnip, cut in quarters

1-2 sweet paprika peppers, left whole

500 g (1 lb 1 1/2 oz) potatoes, peeled

Cube the meat and potatoes into 2 cm (3/4 inch) pieces. Stew the onion in lard over low heat until golden yellow, but not brown. Remove the pot from the heat, add the paprika, meat, salt, and 1 1/5 liters (1 quart 3 oz) water. Add the caraway seeds and peppercorns in a tea ball or a small bag for easy removal before serving the soup. Return to low heat and simmer. After 30 minutes add the carrots, parsnips and paprika peppers. When the meat is nearly tender (around another 30 minutes), add the potatoes. When every ingredient is tender, the dish is done. You can serve it immediately or also reheat when needed.

Serve dried hot paprika on a separate small plate which may be crumbled into the soup according to taste. Fresh white bread is a must with this soup. Goulash sometimes is served in a small cauldron.

BEEF BOUILLON

(Marhahúsleves)

1 kg (2 1/4 lb) beef (brisket, rump,
    sirloin, or shank)

300 g (10 1/2 oz) bone

3 medium carrots

3 medium parsnips

1 small celeriac

1 small kohlrabi

1 small potato

1 small onion

1 clove garlic

1 leave of savoy cabbage, optional

1-2 sprouts, optional

4-5 black peppercorns

Salt, to taste

Cut the cleaned carrots and parsnips in
similar-sized chunks (in four pieces). Wash the
meat and bone then place in a pot in 3 liters
(3 quarts) cold water. Bring to boil and simmer.
When meat is half cooked (total cooking time is
3-4 hours), add all the vegetables and spices.
When the meat is cooked, let the soup settle for
5 minutes then drain and discard the bone, the
onion, the leave of savoy cabbage the
peppercorns and the garlic.

- Cook semolina dumplings, vermicelli or
  small square pasta into the soup.
  Add the other cooked vegetables to
  the tureen of drained soup or serve on a
  separate plate so diners can choose which
  vegetables they want.
  Cut the meat into slices and serve as
  a main course with egg barley (tarhonya),
  steamed rice, or boiled potatoes. Serve
  pickled grated horseradish, mustard or
  tomato or fruit (e. g. apple) sauce in a
  separate bowl.

POULTRY GIBLETS SOUP

(Szárnyasaprólék-leves)

300 g (10 1/2 oz) chicken giblets

1 medium carrot, sliced

1 medium parsnip, sliced

50 g (1 3/4 oz) mushrooms, sliced

100 g (3 1/2 oz) fresh peas

1 small onion, finely chopped

20 g (3/4 oz) lard

Salt, to taste

1 bunch of parsley, finely chopped

Clean and cut the giblets into pieces and start
to cook in 1 liter cold water with very little salt
and cook over low heat until tender, about 30
minutes. In a separate large pan, sauté the
cleaned and sliced carrot, parsnip, mushroom,
the peas and the onion in lard. Add a little salt,
cover the pot. Stir occasionally. When all
liquid has evaporated add the stock and the
giblets, stirring until it boils, then boil for
about 10 minutes. At the end, sprinkle with
parsley.

- Mix 1 egg yolk with 1 tablespoon sour
  cream in the soup tureen and add the
  boiling hot soup, or prepare liver
  dumplings and then add to soup to cook
  through.

BEAN SOUP

(Szárazbableves)

250 g (8 3/4 oz) dry beans
    (pinto or white)

Salt, to taste

1 small onion

1 medium carrot, cut into quarters

1 medium parsnip, cut into quarters

20 g (3/4 oz) lard

40 g (1 1/2 oz) flour

Salt, to taste

A pinch of paprika

A pinch of sugar, optional

Soak the beans in lukewarm water overnight.
Begin cooking in 1 1/2 liters (1 1/2 quarts)
cold water, flavor with salt and peeled onion
left whole. When the beans are almost tender,
add the carrot and parsnip pieces. Continue to
cook for 20 minutes. In a separate pan, prepare
a light roux with the lard and flour (see p. 10),
add the paprika and sugar if desired.
Meanwhile, replace the evaporated water,
(you can tell how much you need to add by
the residue line that is left at the top of the pot
as the soup reduces), then stir in the roux and
boil another 10 minutes.

- Serve with vinegar to flavor to taste. Sliced
  sausage or frankfurter pieces will make
  the soup a tastier and more substantial
  dish. Or add nipped pasta (csipetke)
  to make it richer still.

Using the water in which smoked meat was
cooked earlier will make the soup much tastier,
but then you do not need to add salt to it.

ÓKAI BEAN SOUP

(Jókai-bableves)

00 g (7 oz) dry beans (pinto)
50 g (8 3/4 oz) smoked pork hock (boned)
-2 bay leaves
medium carrot, cut in small cubes
medium parsnip, cut in small cubes
slice celeriac, cut in small cubes
50 g (8 3/4 oz) smoked sausage
0 g (3/4 oz) lard
0 g (1 1/2 oz) flour
small onion, finely chopped
clove garlic, finely chopped
/2 teaspoon paprika
White vinegar, to taste
-2 dl (1/2-3/4 cup) sour cream
/2 bunch parsley, chopped

Soak the beans in lukewarm water overnight, also soak the hock if necessary to take away salty taste. Begin cooking the beans, the hock, and the bay leaves in 1 1/2 liters (1 1/2 quart) cold water (usually, the salty taste of smoked hock makes the addition of salt unnecessary). When the beans and meat are tender, add the cubed vegetables and the sausage, and simmer, adding water to the level where it began (you can tell by the residue line that remains).

After 15 minutes remove the cooked meat and sausage. Make a lightly browned roux from the lard and flour (see p. 10) flavor with onion, garlic and paprika and stir in the soup. Simmer for 10 minutes. Flavor the soup with a little vinegar and the sour cream and simmer for a short time, about 3 minutes. Cut the smoked hock into small pieces, slice the sausage and put them in the simmering soup. Sprinkle with parsley.

This is an imaginative and rich dish, justly named after one of the most famous Hungarian novelists.

Nipped pasta (csipetke) will make the soup more substantial. One or 2 tablespoons sour cream on top of the soup will make it even more appetizing.

POTATO SOUP

(Krumplileves)

400 g (14 oz) potatoes, peeled
20 g (3/4 oz) lard
20 g (3/4 oz) flour
1/4 teaspoon paprika
1 small onion, peeled
Salt, to taste
1 celery leaf, optional
1 medium green pepper, optional
1 small tomato, optional
A bunch of parsley, chopped

Cube the potatoes into 2 cm (3/4 in) pieces. Prepare a light roux with the lard and flour (see p. 10), flavor with paprika, add the potatoes and, stirring, fry for 1 or 2 minutes. Pour in 1 liter (1 quart) water, add salt and the onion, the celery leaf, green pepper and tomato – leaving them all whole – and cook until tender, about 15-20 minutes, adding parsley for the last two minutes.

🥄 Add 1 or 2 tablespoons sour cream or add two sliced frankfurters to enrich the soup, heating through. The onion, tomato and green pepper can remain in the soup when serving, and eaten, if desired.

TOMATO SOUP

(Paradicsomleves)

1 kg (2 1/4 lb) tomatoes
20 g (3/4 oz) lard
20 g (3/4 oz) flour
1 small onion
1 celery leaf
Sugar, to taste
Salt, to taste

Cut the fresh tomatoes in four and cook in 1/2 liter (1 pint) water. When they are cooked 20 minutes, crush the tomatoes in a food mill. Do not use a food processor, because then the peel and seeds won't be separated. In a separate pan, prepare a light roux (see p. 10), stir in the tomato and the necessary amount of water. Add the peeled onion, the celery leaf, the salt and sugar. Cook over low heat for 20 minutes.

▌ *Canned whole, peeled tomatoes may also be used, crushing them in a food mill.*

🥄 Remove the onion and celery leaf from the soup when ready. Serve with croutons on a separate plate or with small square pasta that you cook in the soup during the last 5 minutes. Or add 40 grams (1 1/2 ounces) steamed rice.

HANGOVER SOUP

(Korhelyleves)

20 g (3/4 oz) lard
20 g (3/4 oz) flour
1 small onion, finely chopped or grated
1/4 teaspoon paprika
A pinch of ground black pepper
5-6 dl (2-2 1/2 cups) liquid from sauerkraut
150 g (5 1/4 oz) sauerkraut, finely cut

Prepare a medium brown roux from the lard and flour (see p. 10), add the onion and the paprika. Pour 3-4 dl (1-1 1/2 cups) water over it, flavor with black pepper, add liquid of the sauerkraut, then the sauerkraut and cook to finish.

▌ *Cook with 100-150 g (3 1/2-5 1/4 oz) sliced sausage.*
Excellent cure for hangovers, which explains the name.

(Photo)

HARVEST SOUP

(Kaszásleves)

300 g (10 1/2 oz) smoked pork hock
   (boned)

1 small onion

2 cloves garlic

20 g (3/4 oz) flour

1 dl (1/2 cup) sour cream

A pinch of paprika, optional

1 teaspoon vinegar

1 egg yolk

Cut the well cleaned and presoaked pork hock into large pieces and cook in 1 1/2 liters (1 1/2 quart) water with the peeled onion and garlic in a covered pot, leaving it slightly askew to allow it not to boil over. When the hock is tender remove the onion and garlic. Add some water if you want to extend the soup. Meanwhile, mix the flour with the sour cream and the paprika together in a separate bowl and thicken the soup with it (see p. 10), then flavor with vinegar. Pour in the egg yolk mixed with a little hot soup.

Serve with croutons on a separate plate.

Do not add salt because the smoked meat is salty.

ROUX SOUP

(Rántott leves)

20 g (3/4 oz) lard

20 g (3/4 oz) flour

Salt, to taste

Prepare a dark roux from the lard and flour (see p. 10) and pour 1 liter (1 quart) water over it. Add salt and simmer for 10 minutes.

Use food flavoring instead of salt.

Serve with croutons on a separate plate or, beat an egg in a separate bowl and stir with a fork into the simmering soup until the thread-like egg bits harden.

Nursing mothers used to eat roux soup several times a day because it was believed to enhance lactation. The sick, if they had fever, were also given this soup.

SOUR SOUP WITH EGGS

(Savanyú tojásleves)

20 g (3/4 oz) lard

20 g (3/4 oz) flour

1 small onion, finely chopped

Pinch of sugar

Pinch of paprika

2 bay leaves

Salt, to taste

4 eggs

Approximately 1 tablespoon vinegar

Prepare a dark roux from the lard and flour (see p. 10), flavor with the onion, sugar, and paprika. Add a good 1 liter (1 quart) water, the bay leaves and salt. Bring the soup to boil and simmer for 15 minutes. Carefully break the eggs one by one into the soup so that they stay in one. When the egg whites harden, add the vinegar to taste.

CARAWAY-SEED SOUP

(Köménymagos leves)

20 g (3/4 oz) lard

20 g (3/4 oz) flour

1 teaspoon caraway seeds

Salt, to taste

Prepare a dark roux from the lard and flour (see p. 10), add the caraway seeds and, stirring, brown for 1 or 2 minutes. Pour a good 1 liter (1 quart) water on it, add the salt and simmer for 15 minutes, then strain.

Serve with croutons or with egg similarly to the roux soup.

This soup goes well with dishes made with sauerkraut.

MENU

Caraway-seed soup

Székely goulash

Poppy-seed and apple strudel

CURRANT SOUP WITH WHIPPED EGG-WHITE DUMPLINGS

(Ribizlileves habgaluskával)

1 liter (1 quart) currants
150 g (5 1/4 oz) granulated sugar
Pinch of salt
1 dl (1/2 cup) sour cream
10 g (1/3 oz) flour
2 eggs, separated

Cook the washed and cleaned currants in 1 glass of water for 15 minutes then pass them through a sieve. Add 1 liter (1 quart) water, 100 g (3 1/2 oz) sugar, salt and continue cooking. Thicken with the sour cream mixed with flour (see p. 10). Put the egg yolks in a tureen. Beat the egg whites with the rest of the sugar until stiff and, using a tablespoon, scoop dumplings into the soup, cook briefly, then turn them over. Remove the cooked dumplings and pour the soup over the egg yolks. Mix until you obtain a smooth texture, then add the dumplings.

Serve chilled.

APPLE SOUP

(Almaleves)

600 g (1 1/3 lb) tart apples
40-50 g (1 1/2-1 3/4 ounces) granulated sugar
Small piece of lemon peel
Small piece of cinnamon stick
Pinch of salt
2 dl (3/4 cup) sour cream
20 g (3/4 oz) flour

Place the thin slices of peeled apples in 1.5 liters (1.5 quarts) cold water, add the sugar, cinnamon, lemon peel, salt, bring to boil and simmer for about 10 minutes. When the apples are nearly tender, remove the cinnamon and lemon peel. Thicken the soup with a mixture of sour cream and flour (see p. 10).

Generally, fruit soups are a summer dish and served chilled. Serve at room temperature in the winter.

Less flour is needed if you mix in an egg yolk to thicken the soup.

SOUR-CHERRY SOUP

(Meggyleves)

600 g (1 1/3 lb) pitted sour-cherries (may be mixed with sweet cherries)
40-50 g (1 1/2-1 3/4 oz) granulated sugar
Small piece of lemon peel
Small piece of cinnamon stick
1 or 2 cloves, optional
Salt
2 dl (3/4 cup) sour cream
20 g (3/4 oz) flour

Prepared and served like the Apple soup.

Less sugar is needed if you substitute sweet cream for the sour cream in both recipes.

Serve the chilled sour-cherry soup made with sweet cream in a cup and decorate with slightly sweetened whipped cream on top.

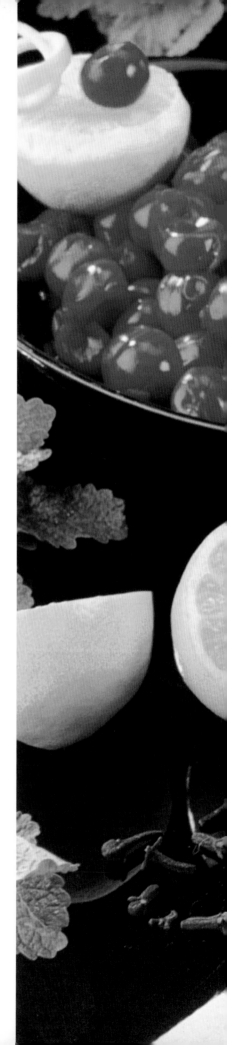

FISHERMAN'S SOUP

(Halászlé)

1 kg (2 1/4 lbs) fish fillets
500 g (1 lb 1 1/2 oz) small fish
1 large onion, thinly sliced
1-2 teaspoons paprika
Salt, to taste
1 or 2 green peppers, diced
1 tomato, diced

Salt the fish fillets. Cook the cleaned small fish and the rings of onion in water that just covers them. Bring to boil and add the paprika. When tender, pass it through a sieve, then add enough water to obtain a thick soup. Add the green peppers and the tomato. Place the fish fillets into the soup with the salt, and simmer for another 20 or 30 minutes.

A good fisherman's soup is made from several kinds of fish. Carp, catfish, sturgeon, pike-perch and bream are the most commonly used in Hungary.

There are many regional variations of this fish soup, but all of them are thick and can be a meal in themselves.

Do not stir, only shake the pot while cooking.

Serve by carefully removing the fish fillets with a skimmer and placing them in the plates, then ladle the soup over them. The best fisherman's soup is cooked in a cauldron over an open fire therefore is this soup served in small cauldrons at the table sometimes.

Serve crumbled, dried red pepper on a separate plate along with the soup, or sprinkle the soup with rings of hot green pepper.

Always serve the soup with fresh white bread.

MENU

Fisherman's soup

Cottage-cheese noodles

with bacon and sour cream

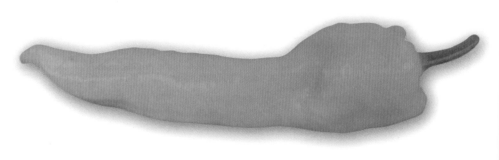

SEMOLINA GNOCCHI I

(Daragaluska)

1 egg, separated

20 g (3/4 oz) lard

40-50 g (1 1/2-1 3/4 oz) semolina

With a fork, mix the egg yolk with the lard, fold in the stiff whipped egg white then lightly mix with enough semolina to obtain a rather soft dough. Dip a teaspoon in the simmering soup and scoop spoonfuls of dough into the soup to cook immediately.

SEMOLINA GNOCCHI II

1 egg, separated

40-50 g (1 1/2-1 3/4 oz) semolina

Beat the egg white until stiff, mix in the egg yolk carefully, and add enough semolina to obtain a rather soft dough. Cook as above.

When the dumplings have grown, check the center of one to see if they are completely cooked. Dumplings absorb a lot of liquid which is why they are usually cooked separately in stock.

They are a favorite in bouillon.

VERMICELLI, SQUARE AND MULBERRY-LEAF PASTA

(Cérnametélt, kockatészta, eperlevél)

1 egg

100 g (3 1/2 ounces) flour

Salt, to taste

Mix the egg and the flour with a pinch of salt to make a stiff dough (do not add water!), make a round loaf, and allow to rest for 10 or 15 minutes. Without flouring, roll out the dough into a very thin sheet, let it dry slightly. Roll it on the rolling pin, cut it lengthwise, then cut in the desired shape: using a sharp knife, cut into threadlike strips (vermicelli), small squares or a little bigger squares with a pastry cutting wheel (mulberry-leaf). Cook in simmering soup.

Nowadays pasta is seldom made at home since there is a great variety of ready-made pasta available in stores.

NIPPED PASTA

(Csipetke)

---

1 egg

100 g (3 1/2 ounces) flour

Salt

Prepare a stiff dough (as for the vermicelli), roll it out to a 2-3 mm (1/10 in) thickness and pinch fingernail size or smaller bits from it. Cook in simmering soup.

CROUTONS

(Zsemlekocka)

Roll (white bread)

Lard, optional

Cut the roll or white bread into 1 centimeter (1/3 in) or smaller cubes, then, with or without lard, toast the cubes in moderate hot oven. If fried in lard, turn them occasionally with the help of a turner.

LIVER GNOCCHI

(Májgaluska)

---

100 g (3 1/2 oz) chicken or pork liver

1 egg

1 tablespoon fine breadcrumbs

20 grams (3/4 oz) lard

1 teaspoon grated onion

Salt, to taste

Pinch of ground black pepper

1 teaspoon chopped parsley

1-2 tablespoons flour

Cut the liver into tiny pieces, mix with the egg and 2 tablespoons water. Add the breadcrumbs, then set aside to rest for a few minutes. Stirring, fry the onion in lard for about 30 seconds then let it cool. Add to the liver, season with pepper and parsley, and mix with enough flour to obtain a soft mixture. Dip a teaspoon in the simmering soup and scoop spoonfuls of the mixture into the soup. Cook for 2 or 3 minutes.

Add to different vegetable soups, giblet soup and bouillon.

MAIN DISHES

PAN-FRIED SIRLOIN
(Serpenyős rostélyos)

4 slices of sirloin
Salt, to taste
80 g (2 3/4 oz) lard
1 large onion, chopped
1/2 teaspoon paprika
800 g (1 3/4 lb) potatoes, peeled and cut into small cubes
2 green peppers, sliced small
2 tomatoes, cut into small cubes
1/4 teaspoon caraway seeds, optional

Pound the slices of meat slightly, score the edges covered with membrane, salt. Quick-fry the meat on both sides in some hot lard, remove from the pan and set aside. Add the rest of the lard and sauté the onion until opaque. Remove from the heat, sprinkle with paprika, pour in a little water, replace the slices of meat, and braise under cover. When the meat is almost done, remove from the pan, put in the potatoes and place the meat on top together with the green peppers and tomatoes. Sprinkle with caraway seeds, if desired. Add water, cover, and cook gently until tender.

Place the meat on the serving plate first, then pile the potatoes on the meat. Pour the gravy around the edges of the meat. Decorate with thin slices of fresh hot green pepper. Serve with salad or pickles.

KETTLE GOULASH
(Bográcsgulyás)

700 g (1 1/2 lb) shank or neck of beef

1 large onion, chopped

50 g (1 3/4 oz) lard

1/2 teaspoon paprika

2 green peppers, diced

1 large tomato, diced

Salt, to taste

800 g (1 3/4 lb) potatoes, cut into small
   cubes

Cut the cleaned meat into 2 centimeter (3/4 in)
cubes. Stirring sauté the onion in lard until
opaque, remove the pot from the heat.
Sprinkle with the paprika, add the meat, the
green peppers and tomato and salt. Stir for
1 or 2 minutes, add water just to cover the
ingredients and cover the pot. Cook slowly
about 40 minutes, checking occasionally and
adding water to keep it at the same level. Add
potatoes and cook 15 minutes more, until
completely cooked.

*To give even more flavor, cook with black pepper
and caraway seeds in a spice bag, removing
before serving.*

Before serving, add nipped pasta (csipetke)
made from 50 g (1 3/4 oz) flour and 1 egg
and cook for a few more minutes. Serve with
fresh white bread and dried hot red pepper
on a separate plate.

*There are many variations of goulash. For
instance, Goulash Szeged style contains sliced
carrot and parsnip; sliced white cabbage is added
to Goulash Kolozsvár style together with the
potatoes; instead of potatoes, Goulash Csángó
style contains sauerkraut and rice.*

TRANSYLVANIAN BLACK-PEPPER FRICASSE
(Erdélyi borsos tokány)

800 g (1 3/4 lb) round of beef
   (blade, sirloin)

1 large onion, chopped

60 g (2 oz) lard

Salt, to taste

1/2 teaspoon ground black pepper

1 teaspoon flour

1 dl (1/2 cup) sour cream

Cut the meat into strips the size of a woman's
little finger. Fry the onion in melted lard until
it turns opaque. Stir in the meat, salt, and
black pepper and, adding a little water, cook
gently in a covered pan. When the meat is
tender, cook to reduce the liquid, then sprinkle
with the flour and brown. Add water to obtain
a thick gravy. Season, if necessary, and bring to
boil. Stir in the sour cream before serving.

Serve with mashed potatoes, maize
porridge or small gnocchi.

BEEF STEW

(Marhapörkölt)

800 g (1 3/4 lb) shank, blade
  or rump of beef

large onion, chopped

50 g (1 3/4 oz) lard

1-2 green peppers, diced

tomato, diced

Salt, to taste

teaspoon paprika

Cut the cleaned meat into 2 centimeter (3/4 in)
cubes. Sauté the onion in lard until opaque,
add the meat, the green pepper and tomato,
salt. Stir for 1 or 2 minutes, add a small
amount of water, cover and braise until tender.
If necessary, add liquid, but very little at a
time. When half-done, add the paprika and
brown the meat. Add water sparingly to keep
the sauce thick, bring to boil and simmer for
1 or 2 minutes.

*It will taste better if you add red wine
instead of water at the end.*

Serve with boiled potatoes or egg barley or
maize porridge and salad or pickles.

BEEF IN GRAVY

(Vadas marhahús)

800 g (1 3/4 lb) eye of round

50 g (1 3/4 oz) smoked bacon

50 g (1 3/4 oz) lard

2 tablespoons flour

10 g (1/3 oz) sugar

3-4 drops of vinegar

1-2 teaspoons mustard

2 dl (3/4 cup) sour cream

For the marinade

100 g (3 1/2 oz) carrots, cleaned, sliced

100 g (3 1/2 oz) parsnips, cleaned, sliced

1 small onion, cleaned, sliced

5-6 black peppercorns

1-2 bay leaves

Salt, to taste

1-2 tablespoons vinegar

Remove membrane from meat if there is some. Prepare the marinade: Put the carrots, parsnips and onion into 1 liter (1 quart) water seasoned with black pepper, bay leaves, and salt. Cook until half-done, add the vinegar. Pour marinade on the meat, cover and keep refrigerated for 2 or 3 days covered (turn the meat once in a while).

Remove meat from marinade, drain, cut slits into it and insert small slices of bacon, then roast in the oven one and a half hours adding the liquid a little at a time. Then add the marinaded vegetables. Cook another hour or more until the meat is tender, continuing to reduce the liquid until all the water is gone and only the fat is left.

Remove the meat from the pan, put on a plate, cover, and set aside in a warm place. Prepare the gravy: Sprinkle the cooked vegetables with flour, fry to brown it, pour in the remaining marinade, bring to boil and simmer for a few minutes. In a small pan, melt sugar until it is light brown and then mix with cold water, and stir in the gravy then simmer for five minutes. Flavor with vinegar and mustard, then add the sour cream and stir through.

Arrange the sliced meat on a serving plate and pour on the gravy.

Serve with bread dumplings or macaroni.

VEAL STEW

(Borjúpörkölt)

800 g (1 3/4 lb) boned blade
and knuckle of veal

80 g (2 3/4 oz) lard

1 medium onion, chopped

1 teaspoon mild paprika

Salt, to taste

1 tablespoon tomato paste

1 green pepper, diced

Cut the meat into 2 centimeter (3/4 inch) cubes. Stirring fry the onion in lard until golden brown. Remove from the heat, sprinkle with paprika, add the meat, salt, stir for a few minutes in the hot lard, then mix with the tomato paste, and cook gently under cover. When half-done, add the green pepper and a little water if necessary, taking care that the gravy remains thick.

Usually, the meat will cook in its own juice, so there is no need to add water. Avoid lifting the lid, if possible, this way the gravy will stay clear. Tender, gristly meat will give the gravy body.

🥄 Serve with small gnocchi, or ewe-cottage cheese gnocchi, or egg barley, and salad.

PAPRIKA VEAL STEW

(Borjúpaprikás)

800 g (1 3/4 lb) boned blade
and shank of veal

80 g (2 3/4 oz) lard

1 medium onion, chopped

1 teaspoon mild paprika

Salt, to taste

1 tablespoon tomato paste

1 green pepper, diced

20 g (3/4 oz) flour

1-2 dl (1/2-3/4 cup) sour cream

Prepared like the veal stew above, but cook it more quickly to reduce all he liquid faster. Then remove the pot from the heat, sprinkle the meat with flour, then fry for 3 minutes. Add a little water to make a thick gravy and bring to boil. Stir in sour cream.

🥄 Serve with small gnocchi, or egg barley.

WIENER SCHNITZEL

(Bécsi szelet)

8 slices leg or boned rib of veal (each approx. 120 g [4 oz])	
Salt, to taste	
2 eggs	
100 g (3 1/2 oz) flour	
150 g (5 1/4 oz) breadcrumbs	
Approximately 1 liter (1 quart) oil for frying	

Lightly pound the slices of veal after scoring the edges. Sprinkle with salt and set aside for a few minutes. Beat the eggs with a fork in a soup plate, add salt. Spread the flour on a plate and sift the breadcrumbs on another. Dip first one then the other side of the slices first in flour, then the eggs, and finally in the breadcrumbs. Place immediately in hot oil and deep-fry first one then the other side.

❙ Prepare just before ready to serve. Serve with potatoes, rice, and salad, decorate with a slice of lemon.

❙ *It takes 1 1/2 to 2 minutes for each side to fry to a golden brown color.*
This meat dish was brought to the Austrian Empire – Hungary belonged to the empire at the time – from Northern Italy in the first half of the 19th century and it quickly became very popular in Hungarian territories.

FRIED SHANK OF VEAL

(Rántott borjúláb)

2 shanks of veal	
100 g (3 1/2 oz) carrots, cut in chunks	
100 g (3 1/2 oz) parsnips, cut in chunks	
100 g (3 1/2 oz) flour	
2 eggs	
150 g (5 1/4 oz) breadcrumbs	
Salt, to taste	
Approximately 1 liter (1 quart) oil for frying	

Cook the thoroughly cleaned shanks with the vegetables in salted water to cover until the meat separates from the bone. Drain, remove the bones, chill, then cut thick slices of the skinned, tendinous meat. Dip the meat in flour, egg, and breadcrumbs as described in the recipe of Wiener schnitzel and deep-fry.

❙ Serve very hot with boiled potatoes and tartar sauce.

MENU

Bouillon with vermicelli

Fried pork chops

Rice with mushrooms

French fries

Cucumber salad

Cherry pie

FRIED PORK CUTLETS

(Rántott sertésszelet)

8 slices boned pork chops (each approx. 120 g [4 oz])	
100 g (3 1/2 oz) flour	
2 eggs	
100 g (3 1/2 oz) breadcrumbs	
Salt, to taste	
Approximately 1 liter (1 quart) oil for frying	

Prepared like Wiener schnitzel. Fry one side of the meat under cover and the other side without the cover.

❙ *This variety of fried meat made of pork is extremely popular in Hungary. It is prepared in every household and restaurant.*

❙ Always serve fresh.

FRIED PORK CHOPS PARIS STYLE

(Párizsi szelet)

8 sliced boned pork chops (each approx. 120 g [4 oz])	
150 g (5 1/4 oz) flour	
2 eggs	
Salt, to taste	
Approximately 1 liter (1 quart) oil for frying	

Prepared like Wiener schnitzel, with the difference that flour is used instead of breadcrumbs.

❙ Prepare just before serving.

STUFFED
GREEN PEPPERS

(Töltött paprika)

-10 green peppers (sweet or slightly hot)
00 g (1 lb 1 1/2 oz) leg or shoulder of pork
small onion, grated
0 g (1 3/4 oz) lard
0 g (1 3/4 oz) rice
kg (2 1/4 lb) tomatoes, chopped
0 g (1 1/2 oz) flour
Granulated sugar to taste
alt, to taste

ut the top off the green peppers, remove the
eeds and ribs. Add the onion in 10 g (1/3 oz)
rd and stirring cook 30 seconds. Mince the
eat, mix with the rice, onion, and salt.
oosely fill the green peppers with the stuffing
nd make a hole in the middle with the end of
e stirring spoon so that the rice will have
om to grow. Place the stuffed green peppers
a pot and pour hot, salted water on top to
over them. Cook on a low heat on top of the
tove under cover for 50 minutes. Meantime in
other pot cook the tomatoes with a little
ater and reduce to pulp, pass through a sieve
r a tomato mincer. Prepare a roux from the
our and the remaining lard (see p. 10), stir in
e tomato purée, flavor with sugar and salt,
en pour over the stuffed green peppers and
ook gently for about 10 minutes.

*An easier way of preparing the sauce is to dilute
tomato paste with water to a desired thickness.*

Serve with boiled potatoes.

BLACK PEPPER FRICASSE

(Borsos tokány)

800 g (1 3/4 lb) round of beef
  (blade, sirloin)

50 g (1 3/4 oz) smoked bacon

40 g (1 1/2 oz) lard

1 large onion, chopped

1 tomato, diced, optional

1/4 to 1/2 teaspoon ground black pepper

Salt, to taste

1 green pepper, diced, optional

Cut the meat and the bacon into strips the size of a woman's little finger. Fry the bacon, strain the drippings into another pan and add the lard to the drippings. Stirring fry the onion until golden brown in the lard and bacon drippings, add the meat (and tomato, if used), stir. After 2 minutes add the salt and black pepper and a little water. Cover the pot and braise the meat (when half-done, add the green pepper). Replace the water from time to time. Put the pieces of fried bacon into the dish and cook to finish.

▌ *This is a stew-like dish, but tokány has a very small amount of thick, brown juice.*

🥄 Serve with boiled potatoes or maize porridge and salad or pickles.

PORK STEW

(Sertéspörkölt)

800 g (1 3/4 lb) leg of pork

30 g (1 oz) lard

1 large onion, chopped

1 teaspoon paprika

2 green peppers, diced

1 tomato, diced

Salt, to taste

Cut the meat into 2 cm chunks. Sauté the onion in lard until opaque, remove from the heat and sprinkle with paprika. Add the meat, the green peppers and tomato, salt and stir for 1 or 2 minutes, then cover and let it simmer in its own juice. If necessary, add water, a little at a time.

🥄 Serve with small gnocchi and salad or pickles.

PIG'S KNUCKLES STEW

(Körömpörkölt)

1 kg (2 1/4 lb) pig's knuckles

50 g (1 3/4 oz) lard

1 large onion, chopped

1 teaspoon paprika

Salt, to taste

Cut the cleaned and presoaked knuckles into several pieces at the joints. Melt lard in a deep frying pan until hot, then add the onion and stir-fry until golden brown. Sprinkle with paprika, add the pork and salt, and pour on plenty of water. Cover the pot. Cook until the meat separates from the bones.

🥄 It has plenty of juice. Serve with boiled potatoes and raw sauerkraut.

PORK CHOPS DEBRECEN STYLE

(Debreceni sertéskaraj)

800 g (1 3/4 lb) boned whole pork chop

Salt, to taste

Same length of soft smoked sausage

1/2 teaspoon paprika

1 small onion

1 clove garlic

40 g (1 1/2 oz) lard

Rub the meat with salt and set aside for at least 15 minutes. Using a long thin knife make a hole through the center of the meat for the sausage and put the sausage inside the meat. Sprinkle the meat with paprika and place in a casserole not much bigger than the size of the meat with the onion and garlic beside it. Pour the hot lard over the meat, add a little water and roast in moderately hot oven for about 1 1/2 hours.

▌ *Baste frequently to obtain a nice pinkish tinge.*

🥄 Serve in slices, hot or cold. If served cold, do not add lard; if served hot, pour on gravy made by boiling part of the lard with water.

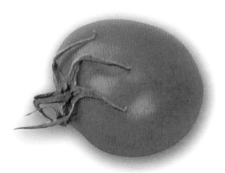

SAUTÉED PORK LIVER

(Pirított sertésmáj)

---

800 g (1 3/4 lb) pork liver

100 g (3 1/2 oz) lard

1 large onion, chopped

1/2 teaspoon ground black pepper

Salt, to taste

Remove membrane from the liver then cut the liver into strips the size of a woman's little finger. Stirring fry the onion in lard until opaque, add the liver, and, continuing stirring, fry for a few minutes. Season with black pepper. Salt only when it is done.

> *It is advisable to soak the liver in water or milk for 15 minutes before frying, otherwise, if the liver is allowed to fry too long, it will turn hard, if too short, it will stay raw inside.*

❚ Prepare just before serving. Serve with boiled potatoes and salad or pickles.

MEAT LOAF STEFÁNIA STYLE

(Stefánia-vagdalt)

---

600 g (1 1/3 lb) leg or shoulder of pork

1 roll

3 eggs (2 hard-boiled)

1/2 teaspoon grated onion

50 g (1 3/4 oz) lard

Ground black pepper, to taste

Salt, to taste

The recipe is the same as for the Oven-cooked meat loaf, with the difference that two hard-boiled eggs are put in the middle of the mixture.

> *1 or 2 cloves of finely chopped garlic may be used instead of the onion or both can be used.*

❚ Meat patties and meat loaves are served hot and cold alike.

OVEN-COOKED MEAT LOAF

(Vagdalt hús sütőben)

---

600 g (1 1/3 lb) leg or shoulder of pork

1 roll

1 egg

1/2 teaspoon grated onion

50 g (1 3/4 oz) lard

Ground black pepper, to taste

Salt, to taste

Shape the minced meat mixture, prepared as below, into a loaf in a casserole, pour on very hot lard and, basting frequently, roast it for about 1 hour in moderate oven. Add spoonfuls of water, if needed.

MEAT PATTIES

(Vagdalt hús)

---

600 g (1 1/3 lb) leg or shoulder of pork

1 roll

1 egg

1/2 teaspoon grated onion

A little lard

Ground black pepper, to taste

Salt, to taste

1-2 tablespoons fine breadcrumbs

1/2 liter (1 pint) oil for frying

Soak the roll in water, when soft, squeeze out excess water. Add the onion to a little melted lard and stir-fry for 30 seconds. Mince the meat, then the roll, add the onion, the egg, season with black pepper and salt, and mix well. Make patties on a board sprinkled with breadcrumbs and deep-fry both sides (not too quickly) in oil.

KIDNEY WITH BRAIN

(Vese velővel)

pork kidney
pork brain
small onion, chopped
0 g (1 3/4 oz) lard
salt, to taste
/2 teaspoon black pepper or paprika

Cut the kidney in half and scrape away the blood vessels. Soak for at least 10 minutes in cold water, then mince. Stirring sauté the onion in lard until opaque, add the kidney, salt, sprinkle with the black pepper and paprika, pour on a little water, and cook for 25 to 30 minutes. Remove the membranes from the brain, cut into tiny pieces, mix with the kidney, and cook until it solidifies. Serve with boiled potatoes and green salad.

ROAST SAUSAGES

(Sült kolbász és hurka)

Fresh liverwurst and other sausages of your choice (but not Italian) are put in an enamel casserole, rubbed with a little chilled lard, then placed in a cool oven. Turn on the heat and, basting once in a while with their own juice, roast until crisp in a hot oven.

These sausages are a favorite winter dish, made in every country household on the days of pig-killing according to a wide range of recipes.

The fresh-roasted sausages are served very hot with sautéed cabbage and mashed potatoes mixed with fried onion. A variety of pickles may be served instead of the cabbage.

(Photo)

JELLIED PORK
(Sertéskocsonya)

1 1/2 kg (3 1/4 lb) pork (feet, snout, ears, tail, head, and skin)

1 medium onion

1 big garlic

10 peppercorn

Salt, to taste (2 teaspoons or more)

Clean the parts to be cooked thoroughly (scrape and singe the skin, wash in several changes of water). Bring slowly to boil all ingredients in 3 liters (3 quarts) water, then simmer over a very low heat for 3 - 4 hours until meat separates from the bones. As water is boiling away, add water to reduced liquid to cover ingredients. When the meat is cooked, remove from the heat and pour in 1 dl (1/2 cup) cold water to clear the liquid. Set aside for 10 minutes, then skim the fat from the surface. Remove the meat and skin from the bones, cut in small pieces, and arrange in a deep bowl or in small dishes, sprinkle with a little salt, and strain the liquid through a cheesecloth to cover the meat. Put in a cool place to jelly (which takes a few hours).

The more skin is cooked, the more easily it jells. Cook and serve 500 g (1 lb 1 1/2 oz) leg of pork with the rest to make it tastier.

Serve as a main course at dinner or as an appetizer.
Sprinkle the jellied pork with paprika.
If served as an appetizer, use a ribbed cake mold. First pour in one inch liquid, let it jelly, cover with slices of hard-boiled eggs, pickled gherkins, sausage. Arrange the meat over these and add the rest of the liquid. When ready, turn the jellied pork onto a platter and serve with lemon juice and pickled horseradish. It will come out easier if the mold is wrapped in a hot towel or submerged in hot water for a moment.

PAPRIKA CHICKEN
(Paprikás csirke)

1 kg (2 1/4 lb) chicken (legs, breast, back, and wings)

50 g (1 3/4 oz) lard

1 medium onion, finely choped

1/2 teaspoon paprika

1 green pepper, sliced

1 tomato, sliced

Salt, to taste

1 teaspoon flour

1 dl (1/2 cup) sour cream

Stir-fry the onion in lard until golden brown. Remove from the heat, sprinkle with paprika. Stir in the pieces of chicken, the green pepper and tomato, salt, cover, and cook gently in its own juice. When the liquid is reduced, brown lightly both sides of the meat, then remove from the pot. Stir the flour in the lard, brown slightly. Pour in 2 dl (3/4 cup) cold water and bring to boil. Replace the meat in the pot. Stir in the sour cream just before serving.

Serve with small gnocchi.

FRIED CHICKEN

(Rántott csirke)

1 small chicken (700 g, 1/2 lb)
Salt, to taste
100 g (3 1/2 oz) flour
2 eggs
150 g (5 1/4 oz) breadcrumbs
1 liter (1 quart) oil for frying

Cut the chicken into pieces. Put the liver and the gizzard between the wing joints. Salt the meat lightly and place on absorbant paper. Coat like the Wiener schnitzel. Deep-fry both sides until golden brown in hot oil, making sure it is cooked through.

Fry the chicken gently over moderate heat under cover at first to cook thoroughly. Be careful when you fry the wing with the liver because it sputters.

When the meat is ready, fry a bunch of parsley in the oil to garnish the platter with. Serve with parsleyed new potatoes and green or cucumber salad.

HASHED BREAST OF GOOSE

(Vagdalt libamell)

1 breast of goose
150 g (5 1/4 oz) leg of pork, optional
1 roll
1-2 dl (1/2-3/4 cup) milk
1 small onion, finely chopped or grated
Lard
1 egg, 1 egg white
1 teaspoon ground black pepper
Salt, to taste

Soak the roll in milk. Stirring cook the onion in a little lard for 30 seconds. Skin and bone the breast, squeeze the milk out of the roll and mince together with the meat (you may add pork). Add the onion, the whole egg, black pepper and salt. Put the mixture onto the breastbone, shape, brush with the egg white. Clean the skin of excess fat, spread it over the meat, and tie a string loosely around it. Place in hot oven, pour on very hot lard, and baste with drippings once in a while. Roast for about 1 hour.

❯ Set aside for 10 minutes, remove the string, and put the hash on a plate. Slice crosswise without the bone.
Serve with mashed potatoes and salad or stewed lentils or mashed potatoes with onion and sautéed white and red cabbage.

SAUTÉED GOOSE LIVER

(Pirított libamáj)

1 goose liver
1 or 2 cups milk
1-2 tablespoons goose fat
1 small onion, finely chopped
Paprika or ground black pepper
Salt, to taste

Soak the goose liver in milk for 30 minutes, wipe dry, and dice into 1 cm (1/2 inch) cubes. Stirring fry the onion in goose fat to a light color, then add the liver and, stirring carefully, sauté over high heat for 5 minutes. When finished, season with salt and paprika or black pepper.

❯ Serve with boiled potatoes sprinkled with parsley and salad.

PAN-FRIED GOOSE LIVER

(Sült libamájszelet)

1 goose liver
1 or 2 cups milk
Salt, to taste
3-4 tablespoons flour
50 g (1 1/4 oz) goose fat

Soak the liver in milk for 30 minutes, wipe dry, cut into thin slices. Salt both sides, dip into the flour, and fry not too quickly in a small amount of goose fat.

❯ Arrange the slices on a platter and moisten with the goose fat.

(Photo)

GOOSE LIVER FRIED IN GOOSE FAT

(Libamáj zsírjában)

1 goose liver

1 or 2 cups milk

100 g (3 1/2 oz) or more goose fat

Salt, to taste

Remove the heart from the liver. Soak the liver in milk for 30 minutes, wipe dry. Heat the goose fat in a short, casserole-style pot and fry the liver for a few minutes until it acquires a little color, then pour in water to half cover the liver. Cover and cook gently in the oven until all water is reduced. Take off the lid and roast until redish on all sides.

Add a clove of garlic or a small piece of onion while cooking (optional).

A really good goose liver weighs at least 700 g (1 1/2 lb) and has a light, almost white color.

If you want to serve it cold, transfer the liver onto a platter with a skimmer. Strain the dripping on top of the liver, spice with paprika. Allow to cool, then refrigerate. Spread the chilled fat on fresh white bread, cover with very thin slices of liver, and salt. This heavenly delicacy should be served only at informal gatherings.

If you want to serve the goose liver warm, take it out of the pot, let it stand for 5 minutes, then slice.

Slices of fresh fried goose liver (and a few bits of fresh crackling) with mashed potatoes and salad can be served as a main course.

A slice of chilled goose liver, garnished with lettuce and diced aspic, is an excellent appetizer. It may also be served with other chilled appetizers.

Dip the knife in hot water to slice the chilled goose liver.

SERBIAN CARP

(Rácponty)

1 kg (2 1/4 lb) potatoes	
Bacon for larding	
1.2 kg (2 2/3 lb) carp	
50 g (1 3/4 oz) lard	
Salt, to taste	
2 medium onions, sliced into rings	
1 teaspoon paprika	
3-4 green peppers, sliced	
2-3 tomatoes, sliced	
2 dl (3/4 cup) sour cream	

Boil the potatoes in their skin, peel, slice. Cut the bacon into thin strips. Clean the fish, salt, crimp the sides and lard with bacon strips. Arrange the potato slices on the bottom of a heat-resistant, lightly greased dish, then add salt. Cover the potatoes evenly with the onion rings, green pepper and tomato. Place the fish on top, sprinkle with hot lard, and bake in moderate hot oven for 30 to 40 minutes. When ready, pour on the sour cream and reheat.

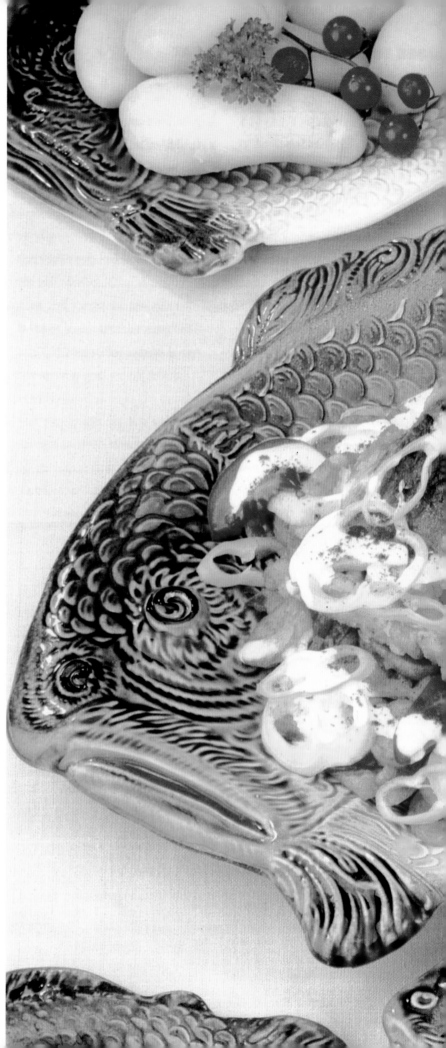

GREEN PEPPER AND TOMATO STEW

(Lecsó)

1 kg (2 1/4 lb) green peppers

500 g (1 lb 1 1/2 oz) tomatoes

2 medium onions

40 g (1 1/2 oz) lard

Salt, to taste

Cut the green peppers in half, core and remove the veins, slice. Cut the tomatoes into quarters (if you want to peel them, poach in boiling water first). Cut the onions into rings and stirring fry lightly in lard. Stir in the green peppers and tomatoes, salt. Cook under cover until limp.

It will enhance the taste if you use dripping of smoked bacon instead of lard.
You can cook slices of frankfurters or slightly smoked sausages, or a few eggs scrambled with salt (and perhaps some sour cream) into the finished lecsó.

Serve with boiled potatoes or steamed rice or white bread.

LAYERED SAUERKRAUT KOLOZSVÁR STYLE

(Kolozsvári rakott káposzta)

1 kg (2 1/4 lb) sauerkraut

100 g (3 1/2 oz) lard

100 g (3 1/2 oz) rice

Salt, to taste

400 g (14 oz) shoulder or leg of pork

1 small onion, finely chopped

1/2 teaspoon paprika

150 g (5 1/4 oz) soft smoked sausage

3 dl (1 1/4 cup) sour cream

Black pepper, to taste

Braise the cabbage in a small amount of lard with a little water, if needed, to make it tender. Lightly fry the rice in a little lard, add water in double amount of rice and salt, bring to a boil and lower heat to a simmer and cook under cover for about 15 minutes. Mince the meat. In another pan, fry the onion in a small amount of lard. Add the paprika, the meat, some salt and pepper and sauté. Stir in the rice. Slice the sausage. Grease a heat-resistant dish, add the ingredients in 3 or 4 layers: first the sauerkraut, then the meat and the slices of sausage, sprinkle the layers with sour cream and the remaining shortening. Finish with a layer of sauerkraut, cover it with slices of sausage, and pour on sour cream. Bake in hot oven for 20 minutes.

STUFFED CABBAGE

(Töltött káposzta)

300 g (10 1/2 oz) smoked pork rib chops

400 g (14 oz) shoulder or flank of pork

1/2 teaspoon grated onion

50 g (1 3/4 oz) lard

40 g (1 1/2 oz) rice

1 kg (2 1/4 lb) sauerkraut

8-10 sour cabbage leaves

Pinch of ground black pepper

Salt, to taste

1 egg, optional

30 g (1 oz) flour

2 dl (3/4 cup) sour cream

Cut the rib chops to pieces along the ribs. Mince the shoulder (or flank) of pork. Sauté the onion in lard until opaque, add the rice and continue to sauté. Pour on boiling water, salt, and cook gently under cover until all water is absorbed. Mix the half-cooked rice with the minced meat, salt, and pepper (you may add 1 egg or a tablespoon very finely chopped sauerkraut). Remove the heavy ribs from the cabbage leaves (if they are too big, cut them in half). Place a leaf on the palm of your hand, put a tablespoon of the meat stuffing in the middle, fold the sides of the leaf over the stuffing, and roll the leaf. Grease a pot with lard and spread half of the sauerkraut on the bottom. Arrange the stuffed cabbages on top, then the pieces of rib chops, and cover with rest of the sauerkraut. Pour on enough water to just about cover the top layer. Cover the pot and simmer for approximately 2 hours. When cooked, remove the meat and the stuffed cabbages. Thicken with the smooth mixture of sour cream and flour (see p. 10) the sauerkraut then add again the stuffed cabbage leaves and the smoked meat.

Make meatballs if there are not enough cabbage leaves. You may leave out the smoked meat, or use the stock of smoked meat instead of water. Every time you reheat it, it tastes better. Add water as needed when you reheat the dish.

It tastes and looks better if you pour sour cream on top before serving.

SZÉKELY GOULASH
(Székelygulyás)

600 g (1 1/3 lb) flank, leg or shoulder of pork
50 g (1 3/4 oz) lard
1 large onion, chopped fine
1/2 teaspoon paprika
1 green pepper, diced
1 tomato, diced
Salt, to taste
1 kg (2 1/4 lb) sauerkraut
20 g (3/4 oz) flour
1 dl (1/2 cup) sour cream

Cut the meat into 2 cm pieces. Sauté the onion in lard until opaque. Remove from the heat, sprinkle with paprika, and stir in the meat and the diced green pepper and tomato. Salt. Cover the pan and, over a low heat, simmer until half-cooked, about 25 minutes. Add a little water if necessary. Stir in the sauerkraut, add hot water to just about cover it. Cook gently until tender, another 25 minutes. Thicken with a mixture of sour cream and flour (see p. 10).

It will taste better if you cook in a piece of smoked meat or cook it with stock, or use dripping of fried smoked bacon instead of lard. Reheating will make it even tastier.

Serve with sour cream on top. Garnish with fried strips of scored smoked bacon or fried sausage pieces.

PAN-COOKED POTATOES WITH PAPRIKA
(Paprikás krumpli or Serpenyős burgonya)

1 kg (2 1/4 lb) potatoes
1 large onion
2 green peppers
1-2 large tomatoes
1 teaspoon paprika
40 g (1 1/2 oz) lard
Salt, to taste

Peel and cut the potatoes into segments, chop the onion, core and dice the green peppers together with the tomato. Stirring fry the onion in lard until golden brown, remove from the heat, and sprinkle with paprika. Add the potatoes, green peppers and the tomato, salt. Cook under cover over high heat, adding a little hot water when necessary.

Add only a little water at a time to obtain a thick sauce. Do not stir, only shake the pot to avoid mashing the potatoes.
Drippings of smoked bacon may be used instead of lard.

Before the dish is completely cooked, add sliced or whole sausage or frankfurters. Serve with green salad, dill gherkins, or pickles.

PAPRIKA MUSHROOM
(Gombapaprikás)

600 g (1 1/3 lb) mushrooms
40 g (1 1/2 oz) lard
1 medium onion, finely chopped
1/2 teaspoon paprika
1-2 dl (1/2-3/4 cup) sour cream
Salt, to taste

Slice the cleaned mushrooms. Stirring cook the onion in lard until opaque, remove from the heat, sprinkle with paprika. Add the mushrooms, salt, and cook under cover, stirring occasionally. When they are done, stir in the sour cream and bring to boil. Serve with small gnocchi or steamed rice.

BOILED CABBAGE WITH MEAT
(Lucskos káposzta)

500 g (1 lb) pork ribs
1 kg (2 1/4 lb) white cabbage
20 g (3/4 oz) lard
40 g (1 1/2 oz) flour
Salt, to taste
Vinegar
Dill or marjoram or caraway seeds
1 tablespoon sour cream, optional

Separate the ribs into groups of two or three and cook in salted water just to cover until half-done, about 20-30 minutes. Shred the cabbage into little finger size lengths and widths and add to the meat. Cook until tender, another 20 minutes or so, then thicken with light roux (see p. 10). Flavor with vinegar and dill (or marjoram or caraway seeds). Add the tablespoon of sour cream, if desired.

SIDE DISHES

SMALL GNOCCHI
(Galuska)

50 g (1 3/4 oz) lard	
2 eggs	
1 dl (1/2 cup) milk	
Salt, to taste	
600 g (1 1/3 lb) flour	

Boil salted water in a large pot. Heat 30 grams lard until it turns liquid, then mix in a bowl with the eggs, milk, and a little salt. Add the flour and stir in water so that you get a semi-soft dough. Stir only so long that the ingredients are loosely mixed. Put some dough on a small cutting board that is dampened and using a wet knife, cut off tiny pieces of it into the pot of boiling water. The dumplings will cook in about 3 minutes until they come to the surface of the water. Strain, rinse with hot water, and mix with the remaining melted lard.

It garnishes stews and paprika dishes, and is also the basic ingredient of one-course dishes.

Do not prepare the dough in advance, you must mix it just before you want to cook it.

TRANSYLVANIAN EWE-COTTAGE CHEESE GNOCCHI

(Erdélyi juhtúrós galuska)

1 serving of small gnocchi (see p. 51)

50 g (1 3-4 oz) lard

300 g (10 1/2 oz) ewe-cottage cheese

1 dl (1/2 cup) sour cream

Make small gnocchi. When they are cooked melt the lard in a pot big enough to hold the gnocchi. When it is hot, add the gnocchi. Stir until warm, then sprinkle with crumbled ewe-cottage cheese and sour cream and serve immediately. (Photo see p. 51)

A one-course dish, or, if you forgo the sour cream, you can use it to garnish veal stew, for example.

GNOCCHI SOMOGY STYLE

(Somogyi galuska)

1 serving of gnocchi (see p. 51)

50 g (1 3/4 oz) lard

1 medium onion, finely chopped

A pinch of paprika

2 dl (3/4 cup) sour cream

Salt, to taste

Prepare small gnocchi. Stir-fry the onion in lard until golden brown in a pot big enough to hold the gnocchi. Add the paprika, pour in the sour cream, and bring to boil. Stir the gnocchi into the sauce and serve immediately.

A one-course dish.

GNOCCHI WITH EGGS

(Tojásos galuska)

1 serving of small gnocchi (see p. 51)

60 g (2 oz) lard

4 eggs

1 dl (1/2 cup) milk (or sour cream)

Salt, to taste

Prepare small gnocchi. Melt 20 g lard in a pan, and add the gnocchi. In a small bowl, mix the eggs with milk (or sour cream), salt, and scramble with a fork. Melt the remaining lard in a pan big enough to hold the gnocchi, pour in the eggs, and stir until they begin to solidify, then stir in the gnocchi.

A one-course dish, usually served with green salad. It may also be served with pork or veal stew.

BOILED POTATOES

(Sós vízben főtt kumpli)

600-800 g (1 1/3-1 3/4 lb) potatoes

Salt, to taste

Peel and cut the potatoes into segments, cook in salted water, strain well.

Always cook fresh.

MASHED POTATOES WITH ONION

(Hagymás tört krumpli)

800 g (1 3/4 lb) potatoes

50 g (1 3/4 oz) lard

1 big onion, chopped

1 teaspoon paprika

Salt, to taste

Peel the potatoes after they are cooked. Fry the onion in lard until light golden color, remove from the heat, and sprinkle with paprika. Stir in the mashed or diced potatoes, salt, and reheat.

PARSLEY NEW POTATOES

(Petrezselymes újkrumpli)

1 kg (2 1/4 lb) new potatoes

50 g (1 3/4 oz) lard

Salt, to taste

A large bunch of parsley

Scrub the new potatoes, cut only the large ones in half, put into melted lard, salt, cook under cover and sprinkle with the chopped parsley.

Do not stir, only shake, to avoid mashing the potatoes.

MAIZE PORRIDGE

(Puliszka)

350 g (12 1/4 oz) corn flour
Salt, to taste
1 tablespoon pastry flour
30 g (1 oz) lard

Heat the corn flour in the oven for a few minutes. Boil 1 liter (1 quart) water in a 3 liter (3 quart) pot, add salt, then slowly sprinkle the corn flour into the water while you keep stirring with a whisk to avoid curdling. When it begins to thicken, stir in the pastry flour, keep cooking for a while, then remove from the heat and set aside.

It is particularly popular in Transylvania where the thickening porridge is stirred, or mixed with a special tool that resembles a rolling pin.

Scoop dumplings with a spoon dipped in melted lard and serve with stew-like (pörkölt, paprika, and tokány) dishes. It is also a one-course dish either served cold with warm milk or hot with cold milk, layered with ewe-cottage cheese, and sprinkled with melted lard.

BREAD DUMPLINGS

(Zsemlegombóc)

3 dry (but not hard) rolls
50 g (1 3/4 oz) lard
2 dl (3/4 cup) milk
350 g (12 1/4 oz) flour
1 egg
Salt, to taste

Cut the rolls into small cubes and fry in lard, then sprinkle with 1 dl (1/2 cup) milk. Prepare a soft gnocchi dough from the flour, egg, the remaining milk, salt and water (see p. 51). Stir in the croutons. Dip a tablespoon into water and scoop spoonfuls of dough into boiling salted water. Cook for a few minutes, then check the center of a dumpling to see if it is completly cooked.

Serve with beef in gravy.

STEAMED RICE

(Párolt rizs)

150 g (5 1/4 oz) rice
20 g (3/4 oz) lard
Salt, to taste

Melt the lard, stir in the rice and fry for 3 or 4 minutes, then pour in water double the amount of the rice. Add salt. Bring to a boil. Cover and simmer over very low heat for 15 minutes until the rice absorbs the water.

Add 1 small onion, and cook with the rice. Discard before serving. Another option is to substitute broth for the water.

EGG BARLEY

(Tarhonya)

200 g (7 oz) egg barley
40 g (1 1/2 oz) lard

Fry the egg barley in lard until golden brown, add twice the volume of salted water as the amount of egg barley. Cover and cook over low heat until tender.

Cook with a whole onion for better taste.

Traditionally served with stew-like dishes.

RICE WITH GREEN PEAS

(Zöldborsós rizs)

Steamed rice dish (see p. 53)
200 g (7 oz) fresh peas
20 g (3/4 oz) lard
Salt, to taste
A bunch of parsley, finely chopped

Put the peas in melted lard, salt, and braise under cover, adding very little warm water when necessary. When cooked, add the parsley and stir in steamed rice.

RICE WITH MUSHROOMS

(Gombás rizs)

150 g (5 1/4 oz) rice
150 g (5 1/4 oz) mushrooms
40 g (1 1/2 oz) lard
A bunch of parsley, finely chopped
Salt, to taste

Cut the mushrooms into very thin slices, salt, and stirring ocasionally sauté in half of the lard under cover until limp. Stirring constantly, sauté the rice in rest of the lard for 3 or 4 minutes in another pan. Add the mushrooms, the parsley, pour in hot water, double of measured amount of rice, and boil. Then cover and, over a low simmer, steam the rice until done, about 15 minutes.

BRAISED CABBAGE

(Párolt káposzta)

1 kg white or red cabbage
40 g (1 1/2 oz) lard
1 teaspoon granulated sugar
1 small onion, chopped very fine
1-2 tablespoons vinegar
1/2 teaspoon caraway seeds
A pinch of ground black pepper
Salt, to taste

Core and shred the cabbage. Melt the lard in a casserole pot, add the sugar, and, stirring, brown to a light color. Add the onion and continue stirring over low heat for 1 or 2 minutes. Stir in the cabbage, the vinegar mixed with 2 dl (1/4 cup) of water and caraway seeds, and braise under cover, stirring once in a while. After 10 minutes, season with salt and pepper. Continue cooking until desired tenderness, another 5 minutes or so.

The white and red cabbage may be prepared separately or mixed.

Braised cabbage is served with fried pork and fried sausages.

CABBAGE WITH TOMATOES

(Paradicsomos káposzta)

1 kg (2 1/4 lb) white cabbage
Salt, to taste
1 medium onion
1 kg (2 1/4 lb) tomatoes, peeled and chopped
40 g (1 1/2 oz) granulated sugar
50 g (1 3/4 oz) lard
50 g (1 3/4 oz) flour

Cut the cabbage into thin strips or shred. Put into boiling salted water and cook together with the onion until tender. Cook the peeled tomatoes into a purée, then rub through a strainer or use a tomato mincer. Prepare a dark roux from the flour and the lard (see p. 10), add the tomato, the sugar then pour over the cabbage, and cook for another 10 minutes.

You can use canned tomatoes instead of fresh ones.

BRAISED SQUASH

(Tökfőzelék)

.2 kg (2 2/3 lb) shredded yellow squash

Salt

0 g (1 1/2 oz) lard

0 g (1 1/2 oz) flour

A pinch of paprika

small onion, peeled

tomato

sweet green paprika pepper

2-3 dl (3/4-1 1/4 cup) curd

A bunch of fresh dill, chopped

Salt the squash and let it stand for 15 to 30 minutes, depending on how tender it is, then gently squeeze out the excess liquid. Prepare a light roux (see p. 10), add the paprika and a little water. Stir in the shredded squash, add onion, tomato and green paprika pepper, and cook for a few minutes. Flavor with vinegar, add the curd and the dill. Salt, if necessary, and cook. If you use sour cream instead of curd, add it when the squash is cooked, and also add a little more water to the roux. Remove the tomato, paprika pepper and onion before serving.

Serve with any meat dish or fried egg.
Serve chilled in the summer.

STEWED SPINACH

(Parajfőzelék)

1 kg (2 1/4 lb) fresh spinach
Salt, to taste
1 roll
3 dl (1 1/4 cup) milk
20 g (3/4 oz) lard
20 g (3/4 oz) flour
1 clove garlic
A pinch of ground black pepper

Discarding the stalks and center veins from each leaf, wash the spinach thoroughly, put in boiling salted water, and cook for 5 minutes, drain. Soak the roll in milk, when soft, press out excess milk. Mince together with the spinach. Prepare a light roux (see p. 10), flavor with crushed garlic, stir in a little cold water. Add to the spinach and add milk to obtain the desired thickness. Spice with black pepper. Bring to the boil and cook gently for a few minutes.

It is served with a wide range of meat dishes or fried egg, and is always garnished with a few boiled potatoes.

STEWED GREEN BEANS

(Zöldbabfőzelék)

1 kg (2 1/4 lb) green beans
Salt, to taste
40 g (1 1/2 oz) lard
40 g (1 1/2 oz) flour
2-3 tablespoons sour cream
Vinegar, to taste
A pinch of sugar
A bunch of parsley, chopped

Cut the trimmed green beans into longish pieces and cook in 1 liter (1 quart) slightly salted boiling water. Prepare a light roux and add to the cooked green beans (see p. 10). Then, add the sour cream and bring to a boil, stirring constantly. Finally, flavor with vinegar, sugar, and add the parsley.

Put a small peeled onion into the cooking water and remove it when the beans are tender. Cook a mild green pepper and a tomato with the beans to give more flavor.

STEWED LENTILS

(Lencsefőzelék)

500 g (14 oz) lentils
1 small onion, peeled
1-2 bay leaves
Salt, to taste
30 g (1 oz) lard
50 g (1 3/4 oz) flour
A pinch of paprika
Vinegar
A pinch of sugar

Soak the lentils overnight. Begin cooking them in cold water, add the onion and the bay leaves, salt, bring to the boil and simmer. Prepare a light brown roux (see p. 10), stir in the paprika, and add to the cooked lentils. Flavor with vinegar and sugar. Remove the onion and the bay leaves when ready.

A traditional dish for the New Year lunch.

This is an excellent garnish with roast, stew (pörkölt), or meat loaf. Serve with pickled grated horseradish in a separate dish.

STEWED SAVOY CABBAGE

(Kelkáposzta-főzelék)

1 kg (2 1/4 lb) savoy cabbage

500 g (1 lb 1 1/2 oz) potatoes

Salt, to taste

1/2 teaspoon caraway seeds

40 g (1 1/2 oz) lard

40 g (1 1/2 oz) flour

1 teaspoon grated onion

1 clove garlic, crushed

1/2 teaspoon paprika

A pinch of ground black pepper

Remove the core and thick veins of the cabbage and cut the leaves into wide strips. Peel and dice the potatoes. Put the savoy cabbage and the potatoes in boiling salted water just covering them, add caraway seeds, and cook until tender. Prepare a light brown roux, flavor with the onion and garlic (see p. 10). Add to the cabbage. Stirring occasionally and adding a little water if necessary, simmer until pulp-like. Add the black pepper.

MENU

Tomato soup

Stewed savoy cabbage with meat patties

Cottage-cheese dumplings

SAUCES

APPLE SAUCE

(Almamártás)

500 g (1 lb 1 1/2 oz) tart apples

Sugar, to taste

A pinch of salt

1 dl (1/2 cup) sour cream

1 tablespoon flour

Core the peeled apples, slice. Pour on water to almost cover the fruit. Add the sugar and salt, cook over low heat until tender. Thicken with the sour cream and the flour (see p. 10).

Instead of apple, use quince, stoned sour cherries, cleaned gooseberries.

Serve warm with cooked meat that has been taken out of bouillon.

TOMATO SAUCE

(Paradicsommártás)

800 g (1 3/4 lb) tomatoes

1 small onion, peeled

Celery leaf

40 g (1 1/2 oz) lard

50 g (1 3/4 oz) flour

Sugar, to taste

Salt, to taste

Dice the tomatoes and cook with the onion and the celery leaf until pulpous. Remove the onion and the celery leaf, then rub the pulp through a strainer. Prepare a light roux (see p. 10), add the tomato juice, and cook gently for 15 minutes. Flavor with sugar and salt.

It is easier to use tomato paste instead of fresh tomatoes.

It is served mainly with cooked meat taken out of bouillon.

SALADS

SALAD DRESSING
(Salátalé)

Water
A pinch of salt
Sugar
Vinegar

Flavor the water with the ingredients to obtain the piquant taste of lemonade.

CUCUMBER SALAD
(Uborkasaláta)

500 g (1 lb 1 1/2 oz) cucumbers
1/2 teaspoon salt
Salad dressing
1/2 small onion, sliced, or 1 clove garlic, optional

Peel the cucumbers, slice or shred very thin, salt lightly, and allow to stand for 30 minutes. Squeeze out the excess liquid (add the garlic or the onion), pour on the salad dressing and chill. If using garlic, remove it before serving.

🥄 Sprinkle with paprika or ground black pepper or finely chopped parsley.

❚ *It tastes best if made from juicy cucumbers.*

GREEN SALAD

(Fejes saláta)

1 lettuce
Salt to taste
Salad dressing (see p. 61.)

Remove the outer leaves, then cut the lettuce in quarters, arrange in a salad bowl. Salt and pour on the dressing just before serving.

❚ Garnish with hard boiled eggs and/or early red radish.

TOMATO SALAD

(Paradicsomsaláta)

500 g (1 lb 1 1/2 oz) tomatoes
1/2 small onion, cut into rings, optional
Salt, to taste
Salad dressing (see p. 61.)

Slice the tomatoes, arrange on salad plates. Add the thinly sliced onion rings, if desire, salt lightly, and pour on the salad dressing.

❚ Sprinkle with ground black pepper or finely chopped parsley.

GREEN-PEPPER SALAD

(Paprikasaláta)

500 g (1 lb 1 1/2 oz) green peppers
Salt, to taste
Salad dressing (see p. 61.)

Core the green peppers, cut into rings, and salt lightly. Allow to stand for 1 hour, then pour on the dressing, and allow to stand for another hour.

❚ *Do not use hot peppers.*

CABBAGE SALAD

(Káposztasaláta)

1 small cabbage (white or red)
1/2 teaspoon salt
Salad dressing (see p. 61.)
1 small onion
1/2 teaspoon caraway seeds, optional

Shred the cabbage, salt, and allow to stand for approximately 1 hour. Squeeze out the excess liquid, flavor with thin onion rings and caraway seeds, if desired. Pour on the salad dressing and allow to stand for another hour.

❚ *You can add thinly cut green pepper rings.*

❚ An attractive dish if you serve half red and half white cabbage on the plate without mixing them.

BEET SALAD

(Céklasaláta)

1.5 kg (3 1/4 lb) beets
1 medium size fresh horseradish, grated
1/2 teaspoon caraway seeds
Salad dressing (see p. 61.)

Wash and cook beets thoroughly. Put into cold water to cool, then peel and slice. Add the horseradish, caraway seeds. Put into a glass jar and pour on salad dressing. Refrigerate to keep fresh for a few days.

❚ *This is a good winter salad.*

❚ The beet slices may be cut into thin strips before serving.

DILL GHERKINS

(Kovászos uborka)

2 kg (4 1/2 lb) gherkins
   (maximum 10 cm [3-3 1/2 in] long)

1 large bunch dill

1 slice bread

2 heaped tablespoons salt

Wash the gherkins, then cut off the ends. Puncture them lightly with a fork in several places. Put half of the dill in a 3 liter (3 quart) glass jar, add the gherkins. Put the salt in 2 liters (2 quarts) water, boil. Allow to cool for a few minutes then pour over the gherkins. Add the rest of the dill and the slice of bread on top of the pickles.

Cover the jar with a plate and put in a warm, sunny place for 3 to 5 days. The gherkins are ready when they turn a yellowish color. Remove the bread and the dill and put the gherkins into a clean jar. Strain the pickling liquid and pour on the gherkins. Keep refrigerated.

You may peel the pickles before serving. Serve them chilled or over ice. They are a very refreshing side dish.

PASTAS

HOME-MADE PASTA
(Házi tészta)

400 g (14 oz) flour
2 eggs
Lard

Sift the flour into a deep bowl, make a depression in the middle, add the eggs and about the same amount of water. Mix with your fingers, then prepare a stiff dough. Put it on a board and continue to knead. Divide in half and cover with cheesecloth. Allow to rest for 15 to 20 minutes. Flour the board lightly and roll the dough into a very thin, round sheet, then tear into irregular, 3-4 cm (1-1 1/2 in) pieces (csusza) or cut into 2×2 cm (1×1 in) large squares. Roll the dough to matchstick thickness to make vermicelli or noodles. Let the dough dry a little before rolling it onto the rolling pin so that it won't stick together. Cut it lengthwise in the middle, then into the desired shape.

Cook the pasta in plenty of salted boiling water. When it comes to the surface, strain, and rinse with hot water. Let it drip, then add to hot but not very hot lard. Lightly stir in various flavorings. Keep the dish warm in a pot filled with hot water until you are ready to serve it.

Use ready-made pasta cooked according to instructions, adding a small amount of shortening into the cooking water (instead of adding the pasta to lard).

COTTAGE-CHEESE NOODLES
(Túrós csusza)

Pasta, torn into irregular pieces
300 g (10 1/2 oz) low-fat cottage cheese
100 g (3 1/2 oz) smoked bacon
30 g (1 oz) lard
2 dl (3/4 cup) sour cream

Crumble the cottage cheese. Dice and fry the bacon. Keep it hot. Add the cooked noodles (csusza) to the melted lard and heat. Pour the noodles into a preheated bowl, stir in the cottage cheese, add the warmed up sour cream, and sprinkle with the bits of bacon. You may also pour on the warm bacon dripping.

Serve as the main course following a substantial soup, or as a dessert, or as a garnish with stewed dishes, in which case, you should leave out the bacon.
Use large square-cut pasta instead of csusza.

It should be served piping hot.

NOODLES WITH WALNUT

(Diós metélt)

Noodles (see p. 65)
20 g (3/4 oz) lard
100 g (3 1/2 oz) walnuts
100 g (3 1/2 oz) confectioner's sugar

Grind the walnut and mix with the sugar. Add the cooked noodles to the melted lard and mix with most of the walnut. Sprinkle the rest on top before serving.

NOODLES
WITH POPPY SEED

(Mákos metélt)

Noodles (see p. 65)
20 g (3/4 oz) lard
100 g (3 1/2 oz) poppy seed
100 g (3 1/2 oz) confectioner's sugar

Grind the poppy seed and mix with the sugar. Add the cooked noodles to the melted lard and mix with most of the poppy seed. Sprinkle the rest on top before serving.

SQUARE-CUT PASTA WITH CABBAGE

(Káposztás kocka)

Large square-cut pasta (see p. 65)
800 g (1 3/4 lb) white cabbage
Salt
80 g (2 3/4 oz) lard
10 g (1/3 oz) sugar
A pinch of ground black pepper

Shred the cabbage, salt, allow to stand for 20 minutes. Melt 60 g (2 oz) lard, brown the sugar, add the cabbage, and stir until browned. Spice with the ground pepper. Cook the pasta adding the rest of the lard to the water, rinse, drain, then mix with the cabbage.

Serve very hot. Some people sprinkle with confectioner's sugar.

SQUARE-CUT PASTA WITH POTATOES

(Gránátos kocka)

Large square-cut pasta (see p. 65)
500 g (1 lb 1 1/2 oz) potatoes
1 small onion, chopped
40 g (1 1/2 oz) lard
1 teaspoon paprika
Salt, to taste

Peel the potatoes, cut into small squares, about the size of dice. Stirring lightly, fry the onion in lard, remove from the heat and sprinkle with paprika. Add the potatoes and salt, cook under cover, stirring occasionally. Add a small amount of water if necessary. Cook the pasta, rinse, and drain, then mix with the potatoes.

SQUARE-CUT PASTA WITH HAM

(Sonkás kocka)

Large square-cut pasta (see p. 65)

250g (8 3/4 oz) cooked, smoked ham

2 eggs, separated

60 g (2 oz) lard

2 dl (3/4 cup) sour cream

1-2 tablespoons breadcrumbs

Grind the ham. Mix the egg yolks with 20 g (3/4 oz) lard, add the ham and sour cream, fold in the beaten egg white. Cook the pasta and add to 30 g (1 oz) melted lard, carefully stir in the ham mixture. Grease a heat-resistant dish, sprinkle with breadcrumbs, and put in the ham and pasta mixture. Bake in hot oven for 25 to 30 minutes.

You cannot substitute the lard with oil. This is a winter meal. Serve with pickles.

JAM POCKETS

(Barátfüle)

500 g (17 1/2 oz) flour

2 eggs, 1 separated

300 g (10 1/2 oz) plum jam

Salt

100 g (2 1/2 oz) breadcrumbs

60 g (2 oz) lard

Prepare the dough with the flour, 1 whole egg and 1 egg yolk. Roll it very thin. Place a teaspoonful of jam every 4 - 5 cm (2 1/4 in) on one half of the dough sheet and make a grid with the egg white between the fillings (work fast to avoid the dough from becoming dry). Fold the other half over and press down with your finger over the grid, then cut with a pastry wheel into squares, following the grid. Cook the jam pockets in boiling salted water until they rise to the surface and are tender (it takes a little longer to cook than the other noodles.) Fry the breadcrumbs in lard until golden brown, then put the cooked, rinsed, and drained jam pockets in it. Do not stir, only shake the covered dish to coat the jam pockets with breadcrumbs.

Sprinkle with cinnamon mixed with confectioner's sugar before serving.

POTATO DOUGH

(Krumplis tészta)

1 kg (2 1/4 lb) potatoes

30 g (1 oz) lard

1 heaped tablespoon semolina

A pinch of salt

200-300 g (7-10 1/2 oz) flour

1 egg

Cook the well washed potatoes, peel, and mash while still warm. Mix with the lard, semolina, a pinch of salt, flour (as much as the potato will take), and the egg to make the dough.

Use the dough immediately.

GNOCCHI WITH POPPY SEED

(Mákos nudli)

Potato dough

20 g (3/4 oz) lard

100 g (3 1/2 oz) poppy seed

100 g (3 1/2 oz) confectioner's sugar

Prepare the gnocchi according to the above recipe. When cooked, add to hot lard, then sprinkle with ground poppy seed mixed with confectioner's sugar.

PLUM DUMPLINGS

(Szilvás gombóc)

Potato dough

Approximately 500 g (1 lb 1 1/2 oz) plums

Cinnamon powder

Salt

80 g (2 3/4 oz) lard

100 g (3 1/2 oz) breadcrumbs

Pit the plums. Roll the dough to 1/2 cm (1/6 in) thick and cut into 8 x 8 cm (3 x 3 in) squares. Place a plum in each square, sprinkling a little cinnamon in place of the pit. Fold the corners over, between your palms make a ball of each square. Put the dumplings into boiling salted water and after they came to the surface of the water cook for another minute or two. Fry the breadcrumbs in lard, add the rinsed and drained dumplings and mix by shaking the covered pan.

If the plum is not sweet enough, put a small lump of sugar in place of the pit. Apricot halves or thick plum jam may be used instead of plums to fill the dumplings.

(Photo)

GNOCCHI
IN BREADCRUMBS

(Prézlis nudli)

Potato dough (see p. 70)

100 g (3 1/2 oz) breadcrumbs

100 g (3 1/2 oz) lard

Divide the dough in half, roll it to 1 cm (1/3 in) thick. Cut it into 2 cm (2/3 in) wide strips, then cut the strips into 1/2 cm (1/6 in) gnocchi and roll them on the board with the palm of your hand. Cook in boiling salted water, rinse well.

Fry the breadcrumbs in lard until pink, add the gnocchi, and mix by shaking the covered pan.

● Serve very hot. Serve with salads, or sprinkle with confectioner's sugar.

NOODLE PUDDING

(Stíriai metélt)

---

500 g (17 1/2 oz) cottage cheese

4 eggs

200 g (7 oz) flour

Salt

3 dl (1 1/4 cup) sour cream

Peel of 1/2 lemon

50 g (1 1/2 oz) butter

2 tablespoons sugar

50 g (1 3/4 oz) raisins

1 tablespoon breadcrumbs

Pass the cottage cheese through a sieve, add 1 egg, the flour, a pinch of salt and 1 tablespoon sour cream to make the dough. Roll it to matchstick thickness and cut into 1 cm (1/3 in) wide noodles. Put in boiling salted water and cook about 5 minutes, or until to desired doneness. Grate the lemon peel. Mix 40 g butter with 3 egg yolks in a bowl with a wooden spoon, stir in sugar and the remaining sour cream. Add the lemon peel and raisins, fold in the whipped 3 egg whites. Stir in the noodles, grease a casserole with remaining butter and coat with breadcrumbs, then add the noodles. Bake in a preheated very hot oven and cut into squares to serve warm.

● Serve as main course after a rich soup. Turn onto a platter, sprinkle with confectioner's sugar, and serve.

COTTAGE-CHEESE
DUMPLINGS

(Túrógombóc)

---

600 g (1 1/3 lb) cottage cheese

2 eggs

100 g (3 1/2 oz) semolina

2 tablespoons flour

A pinch of salt

30 g (1 oz) butter

50 g (1 3/4 oz) breadcrumbs

1-2 dl (1/2-3/4 cup) sour cream

Pass the cottage cheese through a sieve or mince. Add the eggs, semolina and flour, salt lightly. Allow the mixture to stand for at least 1 hour. Form half the egg-size dumplings with wet hands and cook in plenty of boiling salted water. Boil gently for at least 10 minutes. Cut a dumpling in half to see if it is cooked. While the dumplings are cooking, fry the breadcrumbs in butter. Place the dumplings in a heat-resistant dish, sprinkle with breadcrumbs, and pour on warm sour cream.

● Serve fresh, with confectioner's sugar to taste.

(Photo)

CRÊPES

CRÊPES
(Palacsinta)

2 eggs
A pinch of salt
1 teaspoon sugar (only for sweet crêpes)
3 dl (1 1/4 cup) milk
150 g (5 1/4 oz) flour
1 dl (1/2 cup) soda water
Oil for frying

Mix the egg, salt (sugar), 2 dl (3/4 cup) milk, and the flour in a deep bowl. Mix in the rest of the milk and the soda water to obtain a cream-like consistency. Let it rest for at least 15 minutes. If the batter is too thick, add milk or soda water.

Using a pastry brush, lightly oil the pan, heat, and pour in a small ladle of batter. Gently shake the pan and fry. When the crêpe no longer sticks to the bottom, fry a few seconds more, then turn the crêpe with a spatula and fry the other side.

The recipe is for about 12 crêpes.

MENU

Goulash soup

Crêpes with cottage cheese and jam

CRÊPES WITH COTTAGE CHEESE
(Túrós palacsinta)

12 crêpes
350 g (12 1/4 oz) low-fat cottage cheese
A piece of lemon peel, grated
1 egg, separated
3-4 tablespoons sour cream
50 g (1 3/4 oz) confectioner's sugar
Butter to grease pan

Pass the cottage cheese through a sieve. Beat the egg white until stiff. Add 1 tablespoon sour cream to the cottage cheese, stir in the lemon peel, the egg yolk, and sugar, then fold in the egg white. Spread the filling on the crêpes, roll, put them in greased (with butter) heat-resistant dish. Sprinkle with the sour cream. Put in hot oven for about 10 minutes. Sprinkle with confectioner's sugar before serving.

Flavor the filling with vanilla sugar and raisins cut in half.

CRÊPES WITH JAM
(Lekváros palacsinta)

12 crêpes
Jam
Confectioner's sugar

Spread the crêpes with not very thick jam (apricot is best), roll or fold, sprinkle with sugar, and serve hot.

CRÊPES WITH WALNUT FILLING

(Diós palacsinta)

---

12 crêpes

A piece of lemon peel, grated

2-3 tablespoons confectioner's sugar

200 g (7 oz) ground walnuts

Add the lemon peel mixed with sugar to the walnut. Sprinkle the filling in a line on the crêpes, fold, sprinkle with sugar and serve hot.

Serve the crêpes with cottage cheese, jam, and walnut as a main course after a substantial soup, or as a dessert.

CRÊPES GUNDEL STYLE

(Gundel-palacsinta)

---

12 crêpes

For the filling

200 g (7 oz) ground walnuts

2-3 tablespoons confectioner's sugar

1 dl (1/2 cup) milk

For the sauce

2 tablespoons grated cooking chocolate

1 tablespoon confectioner's sugar

1-2 tablespoons milk

20 g (3/4 oz) butter

2-3 tablespoons rum

For the filling mix the walnut with sugar in a pot, add the hot milk, and, stirring, cook for a few minutes until cream-like. Spread on the crêpes, fold and arrange on a platter.

For the sauce, mix the chocolate with the sugar, add the milk, and cook in a pot over low heat, stirring into a thick sauce. Remove from the heat, add the butter and the rum, stir until smooth.

Pour the chocolate sauce over the hot crêpes filled with walnut. Serve immediately.

Sprinkle with 1-2 tablespoons cognac and serve flambéed.

This dessert, a creation of Károly Gundel, one of the famous restaurateur dynasty in Budapest, crowns any festive dinner.

(Photo)

CRÊPES HORTOBÁGY STYLE
(Hortobágyi palacsinta)

12 crêpes made without sugar (see p. 74)

Paprika Chicken made from
1 small chicken (see p. 38)

A bunch of parsley, finely chopped

A pinch of ground black pepper

Salt, to taste

Shortening to grease the pan

Braise the Paprika Chicken until very tender. Remove the meat from the sauce. Remove the skin and the bones, mince the meat. Mix with enough sauce to obtain a paste. Flavor with parsley and ground pepper. Add salt if desired. Spread the filling on the crêpes, fold (or roll, tucking in the ends). Put the crêpes in lightly greased heat-resistant dish, pour the remaining sauce over them, and reheat in hot oven.

Decorate with slices of green pepper and tomato, sprinkle with sour cream before serving.
Served as an appetizer.

BAKED AND FRIED GOODS

GOLDEN DUMPLINGS

(Aranygaluska)

20 g (3/4 oz) yeast
3 dl (1 1/4 cup) milk
200 g (7 oz) sugar
500 g (17 1/2 oz) flour
2 egg yolks
140 g (5 oz) butter
A pinch of salt
200 g (7 oz) ground walnuts

Use a mug to prepare the leavening agent by crumbling the yeast into 1 dl (1/2 cup) lukewarm milk, adding 1/2 teaspoon sugar. Mix with 3 tablespoons flour to obtain a smooth mixture. Sprinkle with 1/2 teaspoon flour, cover with a cheesecloth and put in a warm place (max. 35°C [95°F]) to raise to twice its size. In a bowl whisk the egg yolks with 50 g (1 3/4 oz) sugar, add rest of the lukewarm milk with the salt.

Sift the rest of the flour (also lukewarm) into another deep bowl, depress in the middle, add the leavening agent, and the milk and egg mixture. Beat the dough with a wooden spoon or a mixer until bubbly, add 60 g (2 oz) lukewarm melted butter, mix well. Raise again in a draft free warm place for 1 hour. Mix the walnut with the remaining sugar. When the dough is ready, turn onto a floured board, knead gently, roll to 1 cm (1/3 in) thickness and cut into small pieces with a biscuit-cutter, like dumplings.

Butter a deep cake pan and cover the bottom with a layer of dumplings, spread with lukewarm melted butter, sprinkle with the walnut-sugar mixture, add another layer of dumplings, and so on, filling the pan two-thirds full. Cover and raise again for about 1 hour. When it is raised twice its size, bake in moderate hot oven for about 1 hour.

Turn onto a platter and serve hot with vanilla sauce.

FRIED DOUGH

(Lángos)

2 medium potatoes
3-4 dl (1 1/4-1 2/3 cups) milk
30 g (1 oz) yeast
A pinch of sugar
400 g (14 oz) flour
1/2 teaspoon salt
1 liter (1 quart) oil

Cook the well-washed potatoes. In a mug, prepare the leavening agent: crumble the yeast into 1 dl (1/2 cup) lukewarm milk, add the sugar, and mix with a little flour. Sprinkle the top with 1/2 teaspoon flour, cover with a cheesecloth and at warm room temperature, let it raise. Peel and mash the potatoes. Sift rest of the flour into a deep bowl, depress in the middle and pour in the leavening agent. Add the still warm mashed potatoes, 1 tablespoon oil, and lukewarm salted milk to make a medium stiff dough, then beat with a wooden spoon or mixer until bubbly. Sprinkle the top with 1/2 teaspoon flour, cover with a cheescloth and put in a similary dry, warm place for about an hour to raise to twice its size. Tear pieces of the dough and pull them thin, palm-size. Put them in plenty of very hot oil and fry one side under cover, remove the cover and fry the other side until crispy.

This is a popular snack sprinkled with salt or rubbed with garlic, and is often sold in markets and at fairs. It can also be served for supper.

RIBBONED DOUGHNUTS

(Szalagos fánk)

Approximately 1/2 l (2 cups) milk
1 tablespoon sugar
20 g (3/4 oz) yeast
500 g (17 1/2 oz) cake flour
2 egg yolks
50 g (1 3/4 oz) confectioner's sugar
50 g (1 3/4 oz) butter
1 small glass rum
A pinch of salt
1 liter (1 quart) oil for frying

Prepare the leavening agent: Over a low heat in a small saucepan, heat 3 dl (1 1/4 cup) milk until lukewarm. Pour into a mug, then stir in the sugar until it dissolves. Add the crumbled yeast and 3 tablespoons flour, mix, cover with a cheesecloth, and put in a warm place (max. 35°C [95°F]). Raise to twice its size. Whisk the egg yolks with the confectioner's sugar in a deep bowl and add the leavening agent. Stir in the melted lukewarm butter, the rum, the remaining salted and lukewarm milk and the rest of the flour to obtain a soft dough.

Beat briskly with a wooden spoon for 20 minutes or use a beater and mix for 5 minutes. Sprinkle the top with 1/2 teaspoon flour, cover, and put in a warm, dry place (as above) until it is raised to one and half its size. Turn onto a floured board, flatten by hand to 1-1 1/2 cm (1/3-1/2 in) thickness. Cut with a doughnut-cutter or use a glass. Place round pieces on a floured board, cover, and raise for another 30 minutes. Be sure not to leave the dough too long, or you will ruin it.

Fry in plenty of moderately hot oil (so they will float). Do not fry too many doughnuts at the same time because they will grow. First fry the top half of the doughnut in a covered pot, then remove the cover and turn to fry the other side. Use a skimmer to remove the doughnuts and place them on paper towel to absorb the excess oil.

They are called ribboned because there is a white "ribbon" around the golden brown doughnuts. It is traditionally served at carnivals, which is why it is also called "carnival doughnuts." The temperature in the kitchen should be warm and even, and take care that there is no draught. All ingredients, the cheesecloth and the board should also be room temperature.

Sprinkle with vanilla sugar while still hot. Serve hot with thinned apricot jam.

ʿTRUDEL DOUGH

Rétestészta)

00 g (17 1/2 oz) pastry flour
  (and some more for sprinkling)
-2 tablespoons lard
alt, to taste
ʿfew tablespoons breadcrumbs
  (ground walnuts, semolina)

ʿix lard the size of a walnut with the flour in
ʿbowl, using a wooden spoon or your hands.
ʿake a depression in the middle and add
-4.5 dl (1 2/3-2 cups) lukewarm salted water
ʿmake a soft dough. Work the dough
ʿoroughly with your palms, then slam it on
ʿe board several times (for about 15 minutes).

When it is smooth and springy and peels
ʿff the board, divide into two balls, taking care
ʿat there are no folds on them. Grease them
ʿghtly on top with lukewarm melted lard and
ʿover each with a preheated inverted pot.
ʿfter 15-20 minutes cover a large table with a
ʿean tablecloth and lightly sprinkle with flour.

Place one of the balls in the center and roll
out the dough a little. Grease lightly. Placing
your hands under the dough, stretch the
dough with the back of your hands. Walking
around the table, stretch the dough by lifting
and pulling. Keep doing this until it becomes
paper thin and covers the table. Remove the
thicker edge of the dough by twisting it over
your hands, then, adding a few drops of water,
knead again. Let it rest, then stretch.

Let the dough dry for a few minutes, then
sprinkle lightly and evenly with warm melted
lard. Using the tablecloth fold back the dough
hanging down the side of the table.

Lightly sprinkle breadcrumbs (ground
nuts, semolina) on one-third of the dough
sprinkling or spreading the filling over it. With
the help of the tablecloth roll up the strudel.
Grease a baking sheet with lard, place the
strudel rolls cut to length on it, and sprinkle
with melted lard. Bake in preheated very hot
oven to a light brown color.

*Strudel can only be made from flour with high
gluten content ground the year before. If you are
uncertain about the quality of the flour, add a
whole egg to the dough. Make the strudels
broad, loosely rolled. Do not place too close
together on the baking sheet. Slice on the sheet.
Allow the fillings to cool before spreading on the
dough.*

Serve the strudel hot or cold, sprinkled
with confectioner's sugar.

Ready-made strudel dough

Spread a sheet of the dough on a dampened
tablecloth, grease abundantly with melted lard
or oil using a brush, sprinkle lightly with very
fine breadcrumbs (or ground nuts or semolina), cover with another sheet, grease, then
spread the filling in a line, and using the
tablecloth roll the strudel. Grease with melted
lard between the layers and the top as well.

COTTAGE-CHEESE STRUDEL

(Túrós rétes)

Strudel dough (see p. 81)

600 g (1 1/3 lb) cottage cheese

2 eggs, separated

2 tablespoons sour cream

4 tablespoons confectioner's sugar

4-5 tablespoons semolina

A pinch of grated lemon peel

50 g (1 3/4 oz) raisins, optional

Pass the cottage cheese through a sieve, mix with the egg yolks, sour cream, 2 tablespoons semolina and the sugar. In a separate bowl, whip the egg whites, then fold into the yolk and cottage cheese mixture along with the lemon peel and the raisins, if desired. Sprinkle the dough in line with semolina and spread on the cottage cheese filling. Prepare as on p. 81.

SOUR-CHERRY STRUDEL

(Meggyes rétes)

Strudel dough (see p. 81)

1 kg (2 1/4 lb) sour cherries

200 g (7 oz) sugar

3 - 4 tablespoons ground walnuts or breadcrumbs

Stone the sour cherries, squeeze gently. Sprinkle the dough in a line with ground walnuts or breadcrumbs, cover them evenly with the sour cherries, sprinkle with sugar. Prepare as on p. 81.

CHERRY STRUDEL

(Cseresznyés rétes)

Strudel dough (see p. 81)

1 kg (2 1/4 lb) cherries

150 g (5 1/4 oz) sugar

3-4 tablespoons ground walnuts or breadcrumbs

Prepared like the Sour-cherry strudel.

APPLE STRUDEL

(Almás rétes)

Strudel dough (see p. 81)

1 kg (2 1/4 lb) tart apples

150-200 g (5 1/4-7 oz) sugar

A pinch of ground cinnamon

3-4 tablespoons ground walnuts or breadcrumbs

Core the unpeeled apples, grate and stew until all liquid is reduced. Stir in the sugar and cinnamon. Sprinkle walnuts or breadcrumbs in a line on the dough, add the apple filling. Prepare as on p. 81.

WALNUT STRUDEL

(Diós rétes)

Strudel dough (see p. 81)

300 g (10 1/2 oz) ground walnuts

300 g (10 1/2 oz) confectioner's sugar

4 tablespoons sour cream

Mix ground walnuts with sugar and sprinkle in line on the dough. Sprinkle with the sour cream. Prepare as on p. 81.

POPPY-SEED STRUDEL

(Mákos rétes)

Strudel dough (see p. 81)

300 g (10 1/2 oz) ground poppy seeds

200 g (7 oz) confectioner's sugar

4 tablespoons sour cream

Mix the poppy seeds with the sugar, spread on the dough in line, and sprinkle with sour cream. Prepare as on p. 81.

CABBAGE STRUDEL

(Káposztás rétes)

Strudel dough (see p. 81)

1.2 kg (2 2/3 lb) white cabbage

50 g (1 3/4 oz) lard

Salt, to taste

1 teaspoon sugar

1/2 teaspoon ground black pepper

Shred the cabbage, salt lightly, and allow to rest for 30 minutes. Melt the lard until hot, add the cabbage, and braise under cover at first adding a little water. When half cooked (about 10 minutes), remove the cover and fry until yellow. Flavor with sugar and black pepper. Cover the dough in line with cabbage filling, and prepare as on p. 81.

❯ Serve very hot without sprinkling with sugar.

The amounts given are enough for two rolls of strudel.

CHERRY PIE

(Cseresznyés lepény)

50 g (2 oz) butter
   and a small amount for the pan

200 g (7 oz) confectioner's sugar

6 eggs, separated

120 g (4 - 4 1/4 oz) fine breadcrumbs

500 g (1 lb 1 1/2 oz) stoned cherries

Beat the butter and half of the sugar with the egg yolks and stir until fluffy and airy. In another bowl, beat the egg whites with the other half of the sugar until stiff. Fold alternately the beaten egg whites and the breadcrumbs into the egg yolk mixture. Stir lightly. Grease the baking pan and pour in the dough. Cover with the drained cherries, pressing them lightly into the dough. Bake in preheated moderate oven for 25 - 30 minutes.

LINZER TORTE WITH LATTICE CRUST

(Rácsos linzer)

For the dough

200 g (7 oz) margarine

500 g (17 1/2 oz) flour

1 pack baking powder

200 g (7 oz) confectioner's sugar

100 g (3 1/2 oz) ground walnuts

1 egg, 1 egg yolk

1 dl (1/2 cup) milk

A pinch of grated lemon peel

A pinch of ground cinnamon

For the filling

150 g (5 1/4 oz) apricot or plum jam

On a large flat surface or on pastry board, mix the margarine with flour and baking powder with your fingers, add the sugar, walnuts, egg, milk, and flavorings. Knead quickly. Leave to stand in a cool place for 30 minutes. Roll out two-thirds of the dough, place in the baking pan, and spread with the jam. Roll the rest of the dough into thin strips and arrange on the jam to form a lattice. Brush with the egg yolk. Bake in preheated moderate oven for 20 or 25 minutes.

▌ *Allow to cool before cutting.*

TURNOVER PIE

(Vargabéles)

Vermicelli made from 300 g (10 1/2 oz) flour
Salt
Strudel dough made from 200 g (7 oz) flour
500 g (17 1/2 oz) low-fat cottage cheese
4 eggs, separated
1 pack vanilla sugar
150 g (5 1/4 oz) confectioner's sugar
2-3 dl (3/4-1 1/4 cup) sour cream
50 g (1 3/4 oz) raisins
50 g (1 3/4 oz) butter

Cook, rinse and drain the vermicelli (see p. 24). Pass the cottage cheese through a sieve (or mince). Mix the egg yolks with the vanilla sugar and sugar, add to the cottage cheese together with the sour cream to obtain a soft filling. Add the raisins, fold in the whipped egg whites and the vermicelli. Butter a large baking pan and line with 3 - 4 layers of strudel dough (see p. 81). Brush with melted butter between the layers. Spread the cottage cheese/ vermicelli filling and cover with the remaining strudel sheets sprinkled with the rest of the melted butter. Bake in preheated moderate hot oven.

Instead of making the two kinds of dough yourself, buy a small pack of strudel sheets and 300 g (10 1/2 oz) vermicelli (made for soups).

After removing the turnover pie from the oven, allow to stand for 15 to 20 minutes. Cut into large squares, sprinkle with confectioner's sugar, and serve on a pastry platter.

GERBEAUD CAKE

(Gerbeaud-szelet)

For the dough
10 g (1/3 oz) yeast
1 lump sugar
1 dl (1/2 cup) milk
350 g (12 1/4 oz) cake flour
200 g (7 oz) margarine
1 egg
50 g (1 3/4 oz) confectioner's sugar
A pinch of baking powder
For the filling
200 g (7 oz) tart jam
120 g (4-4 1/4 oz) ground walnuts
120 g (4-4 1/4 oz) confectioner's sugar
For the icing
150 g (5 1/4 oz) granulated sugar
100 g (3 1/2 oz) dark cooking chocolate
1/2 egg white

In a mug, add the yeast and the lump of sugar to lukewarm milk to make a leavening agent. Mix the margarine with the flour using your fingers on a large, flat surface or on a pastry board. Add the leavening agent, confectioner's sugar, the egg, baking powder, and knead thoroughly.

Divide the dough into three equal parts and roll them out to 25 x 35 cm (10 x 13 in) size. Place one on a baking sheet (it should not reach to the edge of the sheet), spread with jam, then sprinkle with half of the walnut mixed with sugar. Cover with the second layer of dough and again spread with jam and sprinkle with the walnut mixed with sugar.

Cover with the third layer of dough rolled out slightly more to fold over the sides. Allow to raise for one hour at room temperature. Puncture the top. Bake gently until the top is an even light brown color. Slide the cake onto a board.

Leave to cool, then thinly spread the top with jam and the chocolate icing. Make the icing by cooking a syrup from the sugar and 1 dl (1/2 cup) water, add the broken bits of chocolate and stir until it melts. Remove from the heat and continue to stir until it begins to cool and thicken. Stir in 1/2 teaspoon water and 1/2 egg white. When the mixture is smooth, pour on the cake and let it run down the sides. Smooth the icing with a knife.

When the icing hardens, cut the cake into small squares or diamonds.

(Photo)

BEIGLI
(Beigli)

2 dl (3/4 cup) milk
50 g (1 3/4 oz) confectioner's sugar
20 g (2/3 oz) yeast
500 g (17 1/2 oz) flour
250 g (8 3/4 oz) butter (or margarine)
3 eggs plus 1 egg white
A pinch of salt

In a mug, add 1 teaspoon sugar and the yeast to a small amount of lukewarm milk. Mix the butter with the flour using your fingers on a large flat surface or on a pastry board, whisk two eggs and add. Stir in the leavening agent, salt, the remaining milk and sugar. Knead quickly. Cover with cheesecloth and leave to rest for two hours. Divide into two large or four small balls. Roll out into 1/2 cm (1/6 in) thick rectangles, spread on the filling leaving a 1 cm (1/3 in) wide border, roll the dough, and place on a baking sheet with the folded end of the dough on bottom. Brush with a beaten whole egg. Set aside to raise moderately in a warm, dry place for one hour. Brush with egg white and put in cool place for 30 minutes. Puncture the sides lightly with a fork to prevent the crust from breaking and bake in very hot oven for 25 to 30 minutes.

POPPY-SEED BEIGLI
(Mákos beigli)

3 dl (1 1/4 cup) milk
300 g (10 1/2 oz) ground poppy seed
50 g (1 3/4 oz) semolina
200 g (7 oz) confectioner's sugar
1/2 teaspoon grated lemon peel
100 g (3 1/2 oz) raisins
or diced quince jelly, optional

Boil the milk, stir in the poppy seed mixed with semolina, add the sugar and the lemon peel. Add raisins or quince jelly, if desired. Cool before spreading on the dough. Continuing see at Beigli.

> *Do not open the door of the oven while baking beigli. The dough will break if it is too soft (made with too much milk), or if it was raised in a hot place, or if there is too much sugar in the filling, or if there is too much filling, or if the oven is not hot enough.*
> *This is traditionally baked for Christmas, enough to last until the new year.*

WALNUT BEIGLI
(Diós beigli)

150 g (5 1/4 oz) sugar
300 g (10 1/2 oz) ground walnuts
100 g (3 1/2 oz) fine biscuit crumbs
1/2 teaspoon grated lemon peel
100 g (3 1/2 oz) raisins or diced quince jelly

Mix 3 dl (1 1/4 cup) water with the sugar and cook into a thick syrup, add the walnuts. Remove from the heat, stir in the biscuit crumbs and the other ingredients. Leave to cool and spread on the dough. Continuing see at Beigli.

STEFÁNIA CAKE

(Stefánia-torta)

For the dough
6 eggs, separated
6 level tablespoons confectioner's sugar
6 heaped tablespoons flour
plus extra flour for sprinkling
Butter for greasing the pan

For the cream
2 dl (1 cup) strong espresso coffee
250 g (8 3/4 oz) confectioner's sugar
50 g (1 3/4 oz) cocoa powder
120 g (3 oz) butter
Cocoa for sprinkling

Whisk the egg whites with the sugar added a spoonful at a time until stiff. Continue to whisk with the egg yolks added one at a time. Sift the flour gradually and lightly stir in the mixture. Grease with butter and sprinkle with flour the bottom of two cake pans and, dividing the dough, bake six thin layers for the cake, two at a time, for four to six minutes, or until the edges are very lightly browned.

Dissolve the sugar in the coffee, add the cocoa, and, stirring continuously, cook into a thick cream (it is ready when a drop put in water will not run but form a ball). Cool to a lukewarm temperature, then add the butter, and whisk the cream until bubbling (it will also turn a lighter color).

Spread cream on each layer including the top one, then sprinkle evenly with cocoa powder.

DOBOS CAKE

(Dobos-torta)

For the dough

5 eggs, separated

5 level tablespoons confectioner's sugar

5 heaped tablespoons flour
  plus extra flour for sprinkling

Butter for greasing the pan

For the cream

2 dl (1 cup) strong espresso coffee

250 g (8 3/4 oz) confectioner's sugar

50 g (1 3/4 oz) cocoa powder

120 g (3 oz) butter

For the icing

100 g (3 1/2 oz) granulated sugar

2-3 drops vinegar

Butter for greasing the knife

Prepare the dough and the cream according the recipe for Stefánia cake. Set aside one layer of the baked dough, and make the layer cake with the rest of the dough and the cream filling.

Heat the sugar in a pan until light brown, stir in the vinegar, and pour quickly over the layer set aside. Smooth with a warm knife and slice with a knife greased with butter in advance. When the icing hardens, put the top layer on the cake.

You may save some cream to decorate the cake, though the caramel icing looks good enough. You may also use a ready-made cake layers. The cake, named after its creator József Dobos, a restaurateur and confectioner in Budapest, was first made in 1885 and its popularity has not diminished since.

OTHER SWEETS

CHESTNUT PURÉE
(Gesztenyepüré)

1 kg (2 1/4 lb) chestnuts

250 g (9 oz) sugar

1 teaspoon vanilla extract

1-2 tablespoons rum, optional

4 dl (1 2/3 cup) sweet cream

Cook chestnuts until tender, rinse with cold water, peel, and mince with a meat grinder. Make a thick syrup by cooking 200 g (7 oz) sugar, vanilla and a little water. When finished, mix the syrup with the chestnuts. Flavor with rum if you like. Make a stiff whipped cream with the rest of the sugar (you can use more if you like).

Put some whipped cream on the bottom of a large glass bowl or 6-8 goblets, and, using a potato masher, add the chestnut purée. Using a pastry bag, decorate with whipped cream roses.

500 g (1 lb 1 1/2 oz) prepacked chestnut purée will give the same number of servings. Use rum or milk to soften it.

FLOATING ISLAND

Madártej)

eggs, separated
50 g (5 1/4 oz) confectioner's sugar
l (1 quart) milk
stick vanilla
/2 teaspoon cake flour

Whip the egg whites with 3 tablespoons sugar until stiff. Boil water in low casserole-type pot (with a wide bottom) and gently add spoon-ize whipped egg-white dumplings a few at a ime because they grow. Turn them over when hey have grown and cook for 1 or 2 minutes nore. Remove the dumplings with a skimmer nd drain in a strainer.

Mix the egg yolks with 1 dl (1/2 cup) milk, he remaining sugar and the flour. Put the anilla in the rest of the milk and bring to boil, hen pour into the egg yolk mixture, stirring ll the while. Stirring, cook very slowly vithout boiling until it thickens. A good test if t coats a spoon.

Pour the custard in a glass bowl putting the dumplings on top. Decorate with peeled and flaked almond, raisins, grated orange-peel, or diced candied fruit. Serve chilled.

GOOSEBERRY CREAM

(Egreskrém)

500 g (1 lb 1 1/2 oz) gooseberries
150 g (5 1/4 oz) granulated sugar
3 eggs, separated
20 g (2/3 oz) flour

Cook the cleaned gooseberries with 50 g (1 3/4 oz) sugar in 1/4 cup of water. Whip the egg whites with 50 g (1 3/4 oz) sugar until stiff. Mix the egg yolks with the remaining sugar and the flour, add this thickening the goose-berries (see p. 10). Remove from the heat and immediately fold in the whipped egg whites.

Serve chilled in a glass bowl.
Very refreshing dessert especially when it is very hot.

WITCH'S CREAM

(Boszorkánykrém)

1 kg (2 1/4 lb) apples
150 g (5 1/4 oz) sugar
1 tablespoon rum
1 egg white

Bake the apples in very hot oven, pass through a sieve, and, before it cools, add the rum, sugar and egg white and beat until stiff.

Put in a glass bowl or small glass dishes or goblets. Decorate the top with the help of a fork and add berries. Serve with wafer.

Index

Printed in China